THE HISTORY & CULTURE of NATIVE AMERICANS

The
Cheyenne

THE HISTORY & CULTURE of NATIVE AMERICANS

The Apache

The Blackfeet

The Cherokee

The Cheyenne

The Choctaw

The Comanche

The Hopi

The Iroquois

The Lakota Sioux

The Mohawk

The Navajo

The Nez Perce

The Seminole

The Zuni

THE HISTORY & CULTURE of NATIVE AMERICANS

The Cheyenne

SAMUEL WILLARD CROMPTON

Series Editor
PAUL C. ROSIER

CHELSEA HOUSE
An Infobase Learning Company

The Cheyenne
Copyright © 2011 by Infobase Learning

Chelsea House
An imprint of Infobase Learning
132 West 31st Street
New York, NY 10001

Library of Congress Cataloging-in-Publication Data

Crompton, Samuel Willard.
    The Cheyenne / Samuel Willard Crompton.
        p. cm. — (The history and culture of Native Americans)
    Includes bibliographical references and index.
    ISBN 978-1-60413-797-2 (hardcover)
    1. Cheyenne Indians—History—Juvenile literature. I. Title. II. Series.

    E99.C53C76 2011
    978.004'97353—dc22

                                                                2010052644

Chelsea House books are available at special discounts when purchased in bulk quantities for businesses, associations, institutions, or sales promotions. Please call our Special Sales Department in New York at (212) 967-8800 or (800) 322-8755.

You can find Chelsea House on the World Wide Web at http://www.infobaselearning.com

Text design by Lina Farinella
Cover design by Alicia Post
Composition by Newgen North America
Cover printed by Yurchak Printing, Landisville, Pa.
Book printed and bound by Yurchak Printing, Landisville, Pa.
Date printed: May 2011
Printed in the United States of America

10 9 8 7 6 5 4 3 2 1
This book is printed on acid-free paper.

All links and Web addresses were checked and verified to be correct at the time of publication. Because of the dynamic nature of the Web, some addresses and links may have changed since publication and may no longer be valid.

Contents

Foreword by Paul C. Rosier   6

1   No Finer Race of Men   14

2   Early Cheyenne History   20

3   The Cheyenne and the U.S. Government   30

4   Fort Laramie   41

5   Massacres and Migrations   52

6   Custer and Little Bighorn   63

7   Exodus   76

8   Reservation Days   86

9   World Wars and the Great Depression   95

10   The Cheyenne Today   108

Chronology and Timeline   120
Glossary   124
Bibliography   126
Further Resources   128
Picture Credits   130
Index   131
About the Contributors   137

Foreword

by Paul C. Rosier

Native American words, phrases, and tribal names are embedded in the very geography of the United States—in the names of creeks, rivers, lakes, cities, and states, including Alabama, Connecticut, Iowa, Kansas, Illinois, Missouri, Oklahoma, and many others. Yet Native Americans remain the most misunderstood ethnic group in the United States. This is a result of limited coverage of Native American history in middle schools, high schools, and colleges; poor coverage of contemporary Native American issues in the news media; and stereotypes created by Hollywood movies, sporting events, and TV shows.

Two newspaper articles about American Indians caught my eye in recent months. Paired together, they provide us with a good introduction to the experiences of American Indians today: first, how they are stereotyped and turned into commodities; and second, how they see themselves being a part of the United States and of the wider world. (Note: I use the terms *Native Americans* and *American Indians* interchangeably; both terms are considered appropriate.)

In the first article, "Humorous Souvenirs to Some, Offensive Stereotypes to Others," written by Carol Berry in *Indian Country Today*, I read that tourist shops in Colorado were selling "souvenir" T-shirts portraying American Indians as drunks. "My Indian name is Runs with Beer," read one T-shirt offered in Denver. According to the article, the T-shirts are "the kind of stereotype-reinforcing products also seen in nearby Boulder, Estes Park, and likely other Colorado communities, whether as part of the tourism trade or as everyday merchandise." No other ethnic group in the United States is stereotyped in such a public fashion. In addition, Native people are used to sell a range of consumer goods, including the Jeep Cherokee, Red Man chewing tobacco, Land O'Lakes butter, and other items that either objectify or insult them, such as cigar store Indians. As important, non-Indians learn about American Indian history and culture through sports teams such as the Atlanta Braves, Cleveland Indians, Florida State Seminoles, or Washington Redskins, whose name many American Indians consider a racist insult; dictionaries define *redskin* as a "disparaging" or "offensive" term for American Indians. When fans in Atlanta do their "tomahawk chant" at Braves baseball games, they perform two inappropriate and related acts: One, they perpetuate a stereotype of American Indians as violent; and two, they tell a historical narrative that covers up the violent ways that Georgians treated the Cherokee during the Removal period of the 1830s.

The second article, written by Melissa Pinion-Whitt of the San Bernardino *Sun*, addressed an important but unknown dimension of Native American societies that runs counter to the irresponsible and violent image created by products and sporting events. The article, "San Manuels Donate $1.7 M for Aid to Haiti," described a Native American community that had sent aid to Haiti after it was devastated in January 2010 by an earthquake that killed more than 200,000 people, injured hundreds of thousands more, and destroyed the Haitian capital Port au Prince. The San Manuel Band of Mission Indians in California donated $1.7 million to help relief efforts in Haiti; San Manuel children held fund-raisers to collect additional donations. For the San Manuel Indians it was nothing new; in 2007, they had donated $1 million to help Sudanese refugees in Darfur. San Manuel also contributed $700,000 to relief efforts following Hurricane Katrina and Hurricane Rita, and donated $1 million in 2007 for wildfire recovery in Southern California.

Such generosity is consistent with many American Indian nations' cultural practices, such as the "give-away," in which wealthy tribal members give to the needy, and the "potlatch," a winter gift-giving ceremony and feast tradition shared by tribes in the Pacific Northwest. And it is consistent with historical accounts of American Indians' generosity. For example, in 1847 Cherokee and Choctaw, who had recently survived their forced march on a "Trail of Tears" from their homelands in the American South to present-day Oklahoma, sent aid to Irish families after reading of the potato famine, which created a similar forced migration of Irish. A Cherokee newspaper editorial, quoted in Christine Kinealy's *The Great Irish Famine: Impact, Ideology, and Rebellion*, explained that the Cherokee "will be richly repaid by the consciousness of having done a good act, by the moral effect it will produce abroad." During and after World War II, nine Pueblo communities in New Mexico offered to donate food to the hungry in Europe, after Pueblo army veterans told stories of suffering they had witnessed while serving in the United States armed forces overseas. Considering themselves a part of the wider world, Native people have reached beyond their borders, despite their own material poverty, to help create a peaceful world community.

American Indian nations have demonstrated such generosity within the United States, especially in recent years. After the terrorist attacks of September 11, 2001, the Lakota Sioux in South Dakota offered police officers and emergency medical personnel to New York City to help with relief efforts; Indian nations across the country sent millions of dollars to help the victims of the attacks. As an editorial in the *Native American Times* newspaper explained on September 12, 2001, "American Indians love this country like no other. . . . Today, we are all New Yorkers."

Indeed, Native Americans have sacrificed their lives in defending the United States from its enemies in order to maintain their right to be both American and Indian. As the volumes in this series tell us, Native Americans patriotically served as soldiers (including as "code talkers") during World War I and World War II, as well as during the Korean War, the Vietnam War, and, after 9/11, the wars in Afghanistan and Iraq. Native soldiers, men and women, do so today by the tens of thousands because they believe in America, an

America that celebrates different cultures and peoples. Sgt. Leonard Gouge, a Muscogee Creek, explained it best in an article in *Cherokee News Path* in discussing his post-9/11 army service. He said he was willing to serve his country abroad because "by supporting the American way of life, I am preserving the Indian way of life."

This new Chelsea House series has two main goals. The first is to document the rich diversity of American Indian societies and the ways their cultural practices and traditions have evolved over time. The second goal is to provide the reader with coverage of the complex relationships that have developed between non-Indians and Indians over the past several hundred years. This history helps to explain why American Indians consider themselves both American and Indian and why they see preserving this identity as a strength of the American way of life, as evidence to the rest of the world that America is a champion of cultural diversity and religious freedom. By exploring Native Americans' cultural diversity and their contributions to the making of the United States, these volumes confront the stereotypes that paint all American Indians as the same and portray them as violent; as "drunks," as those Colorado T-shirts do; or as rich casino owners, as many news accounts do.

*   *   *

Each of the 14 volumes in this series is written by a scholar who shares my conviction that young adult readers are both fascinated by Native American history and culture and have not been provided with sufficient material to properly understand the diverse nature of this complex history and culture. The authors themselves represent a varied group that includes university teachers and professional writers, men and women, and Native and non-Native. To tell these fascinating stories, this talented group of scholars has examined an incredible variety of sources, both the primary sources that historical actors have created and the secondary sources that historians and anthropologists have written to make sense of the past.

Although the 14 Indian nations (also called tribes and communities) selected for this series have different histories and cultures, they all share certain common experiences. In particular, they had to face an American empire that spread westward in the eighteenth and nineteenth centuries, causing great trauma and change for all Native people in the process. Because each volume documents American Indians' experiences dealing with powerful non-Indian institutions and ideas, I outline below the major periods and features of federal Indian policy-making in order to provide a frame of reference for complex processes of change with which American Indians had to contend. These periods—Assimilation, Indian New Deal, Termination, Red Power, and Self-determination—and specific acts of legislation that define them—in particular the General Allotment Act, the Indian Reorganization Act, and the Indian Self-determination and Education Assistance Act—will appear in all the volumes, especially in the latter chapters.

In 1851, the commissioner of the federal Bureau of Indian Affairs (BIA) outlined a three-part program for subduing American Indians militarily and assimilating them into the United States: concentration, domestication, and incorporation. In the first phase, the federal government waged war with the American Indian nations of the American West in order to "concentrate" them on reservations, away from expanding settlements of white Americans and immigrants. Some American Indian nations experienced terrible violence in resisting federal troops and state militia; others submitted peacefully and accepted life on a reservation. During this phase, roughly from the 1850s to the 1880s, the U.S. government signed hundreds of treaties with defeated American Indian nations. These treaties "reserved" to these American Indian nations specific territory as well as the use of natural resources. And they provided funding for the next phase of "domestication."

During the domestication phase, roughly the 1870s to the early 1900s, federal officials sought to remake American Indians in the mold of white Americans. Through the Civilization Program, which actually started with President Thomas Jefferson, federal officials sent religious missionaries, farm instructors, and teachers to the newly created reservations in an effort to "kill the Indian to save the man," to use a phrase of that time. The ultimate goal was to extinguish American Indian cultural traditions and turn American Indians into Christian yeoman farmers. The most important piece of legislation in this period was the General Allotment Act (or Dawes Act), which mandated that American Indian nations sell much of their territory to white farmers and use the proceeds to farm on what was left of their homelands. The program was a failure, for the most part, because white farmers got much of the best arable land in the process. Another important part of the domestication agenda was the federal boarding school program, which required all American Indian children to attend schools to further their rejection of Indian ways and the adoption of non-Indian ways. The goal of federal reformers, in sum, was to incorporate (or assimilate) American Indians into American society as individual citizens and not as groups with special traditions and religious practices.

During the 1930s some federal officials came to believe that American Indians deserved the right to practice their own religion and sustain their identity as Indians, arguing that such diversity made America stronger. During the Indian New Deal period of the 1930s, BIA commissioner John Collier devised the Indian Reorganization Act (IRA), which passed in 1934, to give American Indian nations more power, not less. Not all American Indians supported the IRA, but most did. They were eager to improve their reservations, which suffered from tremendous poverty that resulted in large measure from federal policies such as the General Allotment Act.

Some federal officials opposed the IRA, however, and pushed for the assimilation of American Indians in a movement called Termination. The two main goals of Termination advocates, during the 1950s and 1960s, were to end (terminate) the federal reservation system and American Indians' political sovereignty derived from treaties and to relocate American Indians from rural reservations to urban areas. These coercive federal assimilation policies in turn generated resistance from Native Americans, including young activists who helped to create the so-called Red Power era of the 1960s and 1970s, which coincided with the African-American civil rights movement. This resistance led to the federal government's rejection of Termination policies in 1970. And in 1975 the U.S. Congress passed the Indian Self-determination and Education Assistance Act, which made it the government's policy to support American Indians' right to determine the future of their communities. Congress then passed legislation to help American Indian nations to improve reservation life; these acts strengthened American Indians' religious freedom, political sovereignty, and economic opportunity.

All American Indians, especially those in the western United States, were affected in some way by the various federal policies described above. But it is important to highlight the fact that each American Indian community responded in different ways to these pressures for change, both the detribalization policies of assimilation and the retribalization policies of self-determination. There is no one group of "Indians." American Indians were and still are a very diverse group. Some embraced the assimilation programs of the federal government and rejected the old traditions; others refused to adopt non-Indian customs or did so selectively, on their own terms. Most American Indians, as I noted above, maintain a dual identity of American and Indian.

Today, there are more than 550 American Indian (and Alaska Natives) nations recognized by the federal government. They have a legal and political status similar to states, but they have special rights and privileges that are the result of congressional acts and the hundreds of treaties that still govern federal-Indian relations today. In July 2008, the total population of American Indians (and Alaska Natives) was 4.9 million, representing about 1.6 percent of the United States population. The state with the highest number of American Indians is California, followed by Oklahoma, home to the Cherokee (the largest American Indian nation in terms of population), and then Arizona, home to the Navajo (the second-largest American Indian nation). All told, roughly half of the American Indian population lives in urban areas; the other half lives on reservations and in other rural parts of the country. Like all their fellow American citizens, American Indians pay federal taxes, obey federal laws, and vote in federal, state, and local elections; they also participate in the democratic processes of their American Indian nations, electing judges, politicians, and other civic officials.

This series on the history and culture of Native Americans celebrates their diversity and differences as well as the ways they have strengthened the broader community of America. Ronnie Lupe, the chairman of the White Mountain Apache government in Arizona, once addressed questions from non-Indians as to "why Indians serve the United States with such distinction and honor?" Lupe, a Korean War veteran, answered those questions during the Gulf War of 1991–1992, in which Native American soldiers served to protect the independence of the Kuwaiti people. He explained in "Chairman's Corner" in *The Fort Apache Scout* that "our loyalty to the United States goes beyond our need to defend our home and reservation lands. . . . Only a few in this country really understand that the indigenous people are a national treasure. Our values have the potential of creating the social, environmental, and spiritual healing that could make this country truly great."

—Paul C. Rosier
Associate Professor of History
Villanova University

No Finer Race
of Men

The Cheyenne are one of the best known of all Indian nations, thanks to their many battles with the U.S. Cavalry and to the many books and films that have the word *Cheyenne* in their titles. Americans of the 1950s and 1960s became accustomed to thinking of the Cheyenne in terms of John Wayne movies and spoofs such as *The Cheyenne Social Club*. Thankfully, the early twenty-first century has brought a more balanced view of the Cheyenne and other Great Plains Native peoples, but there are still inaccuracies and discrepancies to address, beginning with an Anglo-American view of the Cheyenne from the year 1832.

THE TRIBE

In the summer of 1832, Pennsylvania-born George Catlin went west to see and to paint Native Americans. During his trip, he met and painted peoples from the Cree, Blackfeet, Sioux, and Mandan tribes. Only toward the end of his long journey did Catlin meet any Cheyenne, but his short time among them was memorable. He wrote, as cited in *George Catlin: North American Indians*:

> The Shiennes [*sic*] are a small tribe of about 3,000 in numbers, living neighbors to the Sioux, on the west of them, and between the Black Hills and the Rocky Mountains. There is no finer race of men than these in North America, and none superior in stature, excepting the Osages; scarcely a man in the tribe, full grown, who is less than six feet in height. The Shiennes [*sic*] are undoubtedly the richest in horses of any tribe on the Continent, living in a country as they do, where the greatest herds of wild horses are grazing on the prairies, which they catch in great numbers and vend to the Sioux, Mandans and other tribes, as well as to the Fur Traders.

Catlin was accurate in many aspects of this written portrayal. Only toward the end of his description did he add the words that would characterize the Cheyenne to many future Anglo-Americans: "These people are the most desperate set of horsemen, and warriors also, having carried on almost unceasing wars with the Pawnees and Blackfeet, 'time out of mind.'"

This would become one of the more accurate stereotypes, for the Cheyenne were indeed a warrior nation. If chasing the buffalo on horseback was essential to their way of life, so was competition—and warfare—with neighboring tribes. Although the most celebrated Cheyenne battles were between the tribe and the U.S. Cavalry, the Cheyenne also fought with their traditional Indian foes right up to the last quarter of the nineteenth century. Luckily for us today, Catlin painted two of the Cheyenne he met, and these are, quite likely, the first visual depictions of any members of the tribe to have survived into modern times.

HUSBAND AND WIFE

High-Backed Wolf, also called Wolf on the Hill, sits for his portrait, holding a peace pipe recently given to him by the Sioux.

George Catlin's portrait of High-Backed Wolf depicts the Cheyenne chief as a proud and elegant figure.

The Cheyenne chief's elegant face is framed by a thick head of black hair, decorated at the top by a handful of feathers. The face is long, solemn, and unmistakably noble; here, one feels, is the epitome of a Native American leader. There is sorrow in the expression, and though High-Backed Wolf does not look older than 42, one gathers that he has seen much conflict.

His deerskin dress has fringes along the sleeves. These are scalp locks, indicating that High-Backed Wolf has fought in many

Catlin also painted She-Who-Bathes-Her-Knees, the wife of High-Backed Wolf, when he spent time with the Cheyenne on his journey into the West. The shapes painted on her face may have been a part of a coming-of-age ritual.

battles. The Cheyenne were as keen on counting coup (touching an enemy with a lance or a stick) as the taking of scalps, but in this case, the chief's clothing shows that he has conquered and killed many opponents. As strong as the impression given by the painting is, it is surpassed by that of the chief's wife.

She-Who-Bathes-Her-Knees is much younger than her husband: A quick glance suggests that she is 18 or 19 years old. The white calf skin that makes up her blouse is very handsome, and the look is accentuated by blue and red beads set along the shoulders and neck. The young woman has rich, dark hair, parted in the middle, which ends in braids. Her solemn expression nearly equals that of her much-older husband, but it is the facial paint that truly makes her stand out. She-Who-Bathes-Her-Knees has a large red circle painted on each cheek, and both ears are entirely painted in red. There is a red mark where her hair is parted and a large, prominent red cross on her forehead. At first glance, one imagines that the cross has Christian meaning, but there were almost no missionaries among the Cheyenne in 1832. It is much more likely that the cross derives from a Native ceremony, perhaps one that signals her transition from eligible young woman to wife.

The viewer imagines that this husband and wife deeply impressed Catlin. He never saw them again.

TERROR IN THE SKY

A year later, in the autumn of 1833, an event shook the Cheyenne to the core. Thanks to our modern knowledge of astronomy, we are confident that what took place during the early morning of November 13, 1833, was a return of the Leonid meteor shower. To the Anglo Americans of Boston, New York, and Philadelphia, the meteor shower was quite spectacular (one observer estimated that 240,000 different movements were seen in the sky), but to the various Native American groups on the Great Plains—where there were no manmade lights or obstacles to obstruct the light show—it was terrifying.

The Cheyenne believed that the end of the world was at hand. Mothers held their children tight, while fathers and brothers mounted horses and rode out of camp, hoping to strike one great blow (or coup) before the supernatural forces overwhelmed the world. For the Cheyenne, the Night the Stars Fell became one of the most potent, and fearsome, events of tribal memory.

Morning came, and the prairies and hills were still there. The world had not ended, but the Cheyenne were not able to shake their feelings of doom. Even if the gods had not destroyed the world, they surely had something sinister in store for The People, as the Cheyenne called themselves.

George Catlin was one of the first Anglo Americans to meet the Cheyenne. He was not the last. The People of the Great Plains, who had fought the Pawnee and the Blackfeet since "time out of mind" soon faced a new foe, one that came with oxen, cattle, and railroad ties.

Early
Cheyenne History

As Joseph Campbell, the author of *The Hero with a Thousand Faces*, expresses it, heroes come in various guises. Sometimes they appear as tricksters, those who upset the balance of things in order to bring a people to greater awareness. At other times, they come with messages of darkness and doom, as well as words of wisdom as to how a people should survive. One thing they all have in common is an element of suffering: One does not become a hero, a trickster, or a prophet without being singed by fire.

WATER WORLD

Early Cheyenne history is murky, because of a lack of written sources. Thankfully, we have the oral tradition of the tribe, passed down from one memory keeper to another throughout the centuries. In 1967, the Anglo-American historian Margot Liberty teamed with the Cheyenne tribal historian John Stands in Timber to produce *Cheyenne Memories*, a masterpiece of tribal remembrance. According to John Stands in Timber, the very word *Cheyenne* is a blend of the old and the new:

> Their own old name for themselves was *Ni-oh-ma-até-a-nin-ya*, meaning desert people or prairie people. But other tribes had names for them too, especially the first four people that became allied with them, the Suhtai and Arapaho and Apache and Sioux. These four are always mentioned in the early ceremonies of the Cheyenne Sun Dance. But anyway, the Sioux called them *Shi-hel-la,* because the early Sioux misunderstood it when the Cheyennes told them in sign language they were "desert people." They thought it meant they were always using red earth paint on their faces and bodies, so they gave them the Sioux word for that. Then the Sioux changed it to *Shi-hen-na,* and that name was picked up by early white travelers, and it is Cheyenne today.

The Cheyenne did not begin their tribal life in a "desert," but in a watery area on the west side of the Great Lakes. As John Stands in Timber relates it, the early Cheyenne were in another area "where great waters were all around them." The People were very poor at this time, and the slender bows and arrows they made were insufficient for hunting big game, even if there had been any. Therefore, the early Cheyenne lived on fish and small game. How long the Cheyenne lived in that watery world, in what is now Minnesota, is not known, but by the time the first white people arrived on the East Coast (around 1600), the Cheyenne were on the verge of a move to the Great Plains.

The People had a prophet to guide them.

SWEET MEDICINE

"Before his birth the people were bad, living without law and killing one another." This is how John Stands in Timber describes the significance of Sweet Medicine, who is as important to the Cheyenne as Moses is to the Jews and Christ is to the Christians.

No historian or anthropologist has ever been able to date the life and career of Sweet Medicine. It seems safe to say that it was long before the first contact between the Cheyenne and white peoples, whether French-Canadian, Mexican-Spanish, or Anglo-American.

A Cheyenne girl, who was her parents' only child, gave birth to a boy, even though she had not had sexual relations with any man. According to *Cheyenne Memories*, she had a dream in which a voice told her that Sweet Medicine "will come to you, because you are clean, and a young woman." When the baby was born, the girl left her son along the banks of a creek, because she felt unable to care for him (the parallel with the Old Testament story of Moses is uncanny). An old woman (today we would call her middle-aged) with no children of her own stumbled upon the baby boy and brought him to the tent she shared with her husband. Perhaps the elderly couple had also been visited by a voice in a dream, because the man responded immediately, saying that this child would be their grandson and they would call him Sweet Medicine. He was given to young women of the tribe to nurse and grew rapidly, achieving an unusual maturity by the age of 10 (the parallel with the New Testament stories of Jesus's youth is striking).

Sweet Medicine performed his first miracle at 10, changing a hoop into a buffalo calf, which provided meat for the tribe. His second miracle came sometime in his teens, when he chased a sacred bird across hundreds of miles of prairie. Sweet Medicine shot an arrow that pierced the sacred bird but did not bring it down. He traveled from one ridge to another, often being helped by grandmothers in different villages (there is no record of male figures assisting him at this point). Finally, Sweet Medicine located the sacred bird, which had turned into a young man. Retrieving his arrow, Sweet Medicine discovered that it, too, had become sacred and magical; he could travel great distances simply by shooting the arrow from his bow and magically being transported to where it lay.

To this point, Sweet Medicine was a cultural hero, a young man who provided for The People and received their admiration. His personal story, however, took a negative turn and one day—while on his first buffalo hunt—he did something unforgivable that resulted in a long period of exile.

The Cheyenne did not have horses at that point. The buffalo hunt was, therefore, a far cry from what we imagine today. Rather than an exhilarating charge into a herd, and then pursuit, The People had to creep up slowly and carefully, and, with some luck, drive the buffalo into a gully or a ditch to kill a few. Following custom, the elder men of the tribe traveled behind the younger ones, hoping to obtain meat or buffalo skin for a robe. An old man came upon Sweet Medicine, who had felled a buffalo calf, and he asked for its fur.

Sweet Medicine was willing to share the meat, but he refused to part with the hairy robe, and when the old man demanded it as his right, Sweet Medicine reached for a shank and hit him squarely on the head. The old man was not killed, but Sweet Medicine had broken one of the key Cheyenne virtues: hospitality to the elderly. Knowing this, he returned to the village and told his grandmother to be prepared for the men who would come.

They arrived at dusk, angrily demanding that Sweet Medicine surrender himself to them for punishment (what it would be is difficult to say). Sweet Medicine's grandmother acted her part in the drama, according to *Cheyenne Memories*, calling out, "Yes, he is here with me." At the same moment, she tipped the soup into the fire, just as Sweet Medicine had told her. There was a tremendous noise, an explosion, and when the men entered the hut, they found Sweet Medicine was gone. They ran outside and were astonished to see him on a nearby ridge, where he acted several roles in full view:

- He appeared with paint on his body and a stringless bow in his hand.
- He appeared on another ridge, carrying an elk horn and a crook-edged spear.

- Signaling his pursuers to follow, Sweet Medicine appeared again, this time wearing feathers in his hair and red paint on his body.
- For the fourth and last time, he appeared, this time as a dog, with a rawhide rope on the side of his belt.

Then he vanished.

THE SACRED MOUNTAIN

Although The People did not know it, Sweet Medicine had been called by a distant voice that guided him all the way to a striking mountain that the Cheyenne call *Noahvose* (Sacred or Holy Mountain) and that Anglo Americans today call Bear Butte. He entered the holy mountain and remained there for the next four years (four is a sacred number to the Cheyenne and many other Native peoples).

Located in South Dakota, the Cheyenne referred to Bear Butte as *Noahvose,* the Sacred or Holy Mountain. It is connected to the Cheyenne story of Sweet Medicine.

Sacred Land, Secular Use

Bear Butte—the place where Sweet Medicine received his teachings—has been the center of controversies for decades. At the heart of the issue is a question as to whether the mountain is sacred land, and therefore off-limits to development, or merely another bump in the landscape of the Great Plains.

Bear Butte is sacred in the memory of about a dozen Native tribes, including the Cheyenne, the Sioux, and the Kiowa. Its status was challenged in 1961, when the State of South Dakota turned it into Bear Butte State Park. For about 20 years, an uneasy truce existed between the Native people who came to fast and pray and the developers who paved roads in the area and planned to build even bigger. This truce ended in 1981, when the peoples of the tribes received a form letter from the South Dakota superintendent of parks, informing them that they had to obtain five-day permits to go to Bear Butte to fast and pray.

Making matters worse, Bear Butte is only about 10 miles (16 kilometers) from the largest motorcycle rally in the United States. The Sturgis (South Dakota) Rally attracts tens of thousands of people and almost as many motorcycles. In *The Unwanted Sound of Everything We Want: A Book About Noise*, Garret Keizer writes, "To walk the streets of Sturgis by day and especially by night is to feel yourself in the very heart of Loud America, by which I mean, America and all its contradictions played loud." The sounds of Harleys revving up, and the endless near-explosions of gasoline and oil create an environment that does not seem conducive, or welcoming, to the sacred spirit of Bear Butte. Whether the bikers of Sturgis can coexist with the pilgrims of Bear Butte is an important question.

Details of Sweet Medicine's time in the holy mountain are few. Most accounts agree that he was received into the company of Maheo, the master of life, and also met a number of lesser gods and goddesses, whose powers corresponded to the winds and the four directions. The precise instructions that Sweet Medicine received are in some dispute, but there is no doubt that when he emerged four years later, he came with very specific messages for the Cheyenne people. First, however, he had to win his way back into their good graces.

RETURN FROM EXILE

Sweet Medicine acted without fear, presenting himself to a group of Cheyenne children and telling them that he had returned. "Go and tell the people to prepare a tepee for me," he said, according to *Cheyenne Memories*, explaining that he came with a great power, which would transform the lives of the Cheyenne.

Remarkably, the children did just as he said, and when he arrived, Sweet Medicine sang four songs and then called out the words that have remained the cornerstone of the Cheyenne belief system ever since:

> Desert People! Present and future generations of the Desert People! I bring you Sacred Arrows, powerful and holy. The Arrows will make you strong and healthy. They will reform your lives and make you a great nation. They come as the benevolence of your gods!

At that moment, many Cheyenne might have thought it was Sweet Medicine—rather than they—who needed to reform his life. The power of his songs, and the shining way he presented himself, however, could not be denied. In the tipi that The People had created, Sweet Medicine outlined the teachings he had received from the gods:

- The Cheyenne were poor and unhappy because they had offended the gods.
- They had done so by spilling one another's blood.

- They had done so by marrying too closely within their bloodlines.
- These practices must end, and with their end would come the blessing of Maheo.

Much like Moses, who returned from Mount Sinai, Sweet Medicine came from the holiest of mountains. Like Moses, he brought a new set of laws. Unlike Moses, he brought a visual depiction of the supreme god's love and affection. The visual representation was the bundle of Sacred Arrows, four in number.

Holding the Sacred Arrows aloft, Sweet Medicine explained that two were meant to ensure success in the hunt and the other two guaranteed victory in war. Animals would be rendered deaf and dumb by the first two arrows, and enemy warriors would be blind and helpless before the Cheyenne.

Although he had left The People in disgrace and spent years in exile, Sweet Medicine returned as the great prophet, the spiritual leader of the Cheyenne.

TRIBAL ORGANIZATION

Soon after his return, Sweet Medicine outlined a series of important changes for the tribe. The philosophy he brought is described above, but the reforms were very specific. First, Sweet Medicine announced the formation of four warrior bands—the Fox Society, the Elk Society, the Red Shield Society, and the Dog Soldier Society. Each of the four groups had been foreshadowed by his appearance on the ridge on the day his exile began.

The warrior bands became the center of Cheyenne society. Each was to contribute 10 peace chiefs (not warrior ones) to the Council of 44, which would govern The People. The 40 peace chiefs were joined by four other, elder men, who would act as the wisest. No chief would play a dominant role; decisions would be arrived at by consensus among the entire group.

Sweet Medicine did not live long enough to see the introduction of the horse into the Cheyenne way of life, but he did predict major changes for the future. If The People would hold on to their ways, he said, all would be well, but there would be temptations to change. John Stands in Timber describes what Sweet Medicine told The People:

> My friends, once I was young and able, but a man lives only a short time, and now I am old and helpless and ready to leave you. I have brought you many things, sent by the gods for your use. You live the way I have taught you and follow the laws. You must not forget them, for they have given you strength and the ability to support yourselves and your families.

Almost with his last breath, Sweet Medicine predicted the coming of the white peoples (whom he labeled the Earth Men) and the changes that would come about when the buffalo was replaced by cattle:

> But at last you will not remember. Your ways will change. You will leave your religion for something new. You will lose respect for your leaders and start quarreling with one another. You will lose track of your relations and marry women from your own families. You will take after the Earth Men's ways and forget good things by which you have lived and in the end become worse than crazy. I am sorry to say these things, but I have seen them.

The great prophet passed away, and the dire warnings he had issued did not come true for a long time.

TO THE PLAINS

No one knows the precise time that the Cheyenne moved from the western Great Lakes area to the Great Plains. Archaeologists continue to wrestle with this question, but for the moment we have to accept that it happened sometime between 1650 and 1750. What can be said, with certainty, is that soon after the great move, the Cheyenne encountered the animal that would make an enormous difference in their lives. John Stands in Timber describes it thus:

The first Cheyenne who ever saw horses saw them come in to water at a lake, down in the country that is now Wyoming. He went down closer to look, and then he thought of the prophecy of Sweet Medicine, that there would be animals with round hoofs and shaggy manes and tails, and men could ride on their backs.

That first Cheyenne made a rawhide rope, got it onto the horse, and slowly, over the next several days, broke him into submission. The rest, as they say, is history, for the Cheyenne had found the magical animal that would make them masters of the Plains.

The Cheyenne and the U.S. Government

The first white people to meet the Cheyenne were French-Canadian explorers. In 1680, Robert Cavalier de la Salle, who was soon to make his remarkable canoe trip down the Mississippi River, met some Cheyenne in what is now Peoria, Illinois. La Salle did not mention whether these Cheyenne had made the transition from a Great Lakes people to one on the Great Plains, and it may be that The People were in the midst of that great move.

NEIGHBORS AND FRIENDS

From when they first arrived on the Plains, the Cheyenne befriended the people called the Arapaho. As they migrated into what are now Wyoming and northern Colorado, the Cheyenne made allies of the Arapaho, who lived just to the west. The two peoples' languages were similar enough (both from the Algonquian

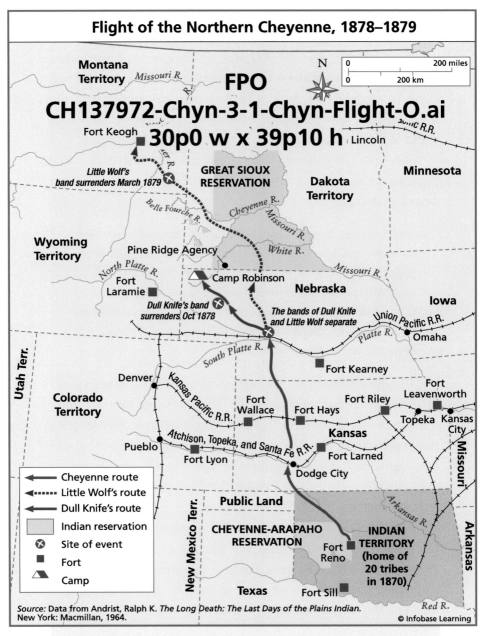

Flight of the Northern Cheyenne, 1878–1879

Montana
Territory *Missouri R.*

FPO
CH137972-Chyn-3-1-Chyn-Flight-O.ai
30p0 w x 39p10 h

N

| 0 | 200 miles |
| 0 | 200 km |

Fort Keogh

Lincoln

Little Wolf's
band surrenders March 1879

GREAT SIOUX
RESERVATION

Dakota
Territory

Minnesota

Belle Fourche R.

Cheyenne R.

Missouri R.

Wyoming
Territory

Pine Ridge Agency

White R.

North Platte R.

Missouri R.

Fort
Laramie

Camp Robinson

Nebraska

Iowa

Dull Knife's band
surrenders Oct 1878

The bands of Dull Knife
and Little Wolf separate

Union Pacific R.R.

Platte R.

Omaha

South Platte R.

Fort Kearney

Fort
Leavenworth

Denver

Kansas Pacific R.R.

Colorado
Territory

Fort
Wallace

Fort Hays

Fort Riley

Topeka Kansas
City

Pueblo

Atchison, Topeka, and Santa Fe R.R.

Kansas

Fort Lyon

Dodge City

Fort Larned

Missouri R.

Utah Terr.

New Mexico Terr.

Public Land

Arkansas R.

CHEYENNE-ARAPAHO
RESERVATION

Fort
Reno

INDIAN
TERRITORY
(home of
20 tribes
in 1870)

Arkansas

Texas

Fort Sill

Red R.

Legend:
- ← Cheyenne route
- ◄······ Little Wolf's route
- ← Dull Knife's route
- ▨ Indian reservation
- ⊗ Site of event
- ▪ Fort
- ▲ Camp

Source: Data from Andrist, Ralph K. *The Long Death: The Last Days of the Plains Indian.*
New York: Macmillan, 1964.

© Infobase Learning

The Cheyenne migrated several times in their history. Originally from
the Great Lakes region of the United States, they eventually moved
into the Plains and the Dakotas. In 1878, after a fight with the Sioux and
capture by federal troops, they were granted a reservation in Montana.

family) that they could understand one another. Both peoples needed, and wanted, allies.

The Cheyenne and the Arapaho became so close that other peoples sometimes mistook them for being the same, but this was never true of the two peoples themselves. They understood the difference and were pleased to have allies in the rather dangerous world of Great Plains warfare.

Soon after they moved onto the Plains, the Cheyenne came in contact with a people called the Suhtai. John Stands in Timber describes it thus:

> Suhtai means "people descended." Their language was nearly the same as Cheyenne, so they could understand each other. Today most Suhtai words have disappeared, but a few still are used. And people remember if they are of Suhtai descent. They claimed they came from a northern country with many lakes, where they got their highest religion. Today most of them are in Montana, and so is the Sacred Hat.

That first meeting of the two peoples—which possibly dates to 1800—was momentous for both. The Cheyenne were far more numerous, and it was clear that any merger between the two peoples would be to the Cheyenne's benefit, as their culture would predominate. The same cannot be said for religion, however; the Suhtai brought a sacred object that is as prized as the Sacred Arrows. This was the Sacred Buffalo Hat.

As the Suhtai merged with and became synonymous with the Cheyenne, the Sacred Buffalo Hat became as important to The People as the Sacred Arrows. Perhaps this was the case because, while the Sacred Arrows were consecrated to success in war and the hunt, the Sacred Buffalo Hat epitomized feminine virtues, fertility most especially. The Keeper of the Sacred Hat went round his campsite each morning, singing of the beauties of the day and the importance of young women keeping their virginity. Practically every Anglo-American explorer who met the Cheyenne in the nineteenth century commented on the extraordinary level of

attention paid to the rituals of courtship and the supreme importance attached to chastity.

By about 1825, the year they negotiated their first treaty with
the United States, the Cheyenne and the Suhtai had merged into
one people.

STARS AND STRIPES

Very likely, the Cheyenne knew nothing about the United States
until captains Meriwether Lewis and William Clark passed
through their country in 1804 and 1805. There were no official
meetings between Lewis and Clark and the Cheyenne, but the two
captains wrote some interesting entries in their journals, describ-
ing what they heard about this ambitious, energetic people who
dominated a large section of the Northern Plains. Lewis and Clark
operated on hearsay when it came to the Cheyenne, but on the
famous map, drawn by Clark in 1810, the captain delineated two
rivers, each of them named "Cheyenne," and there was a large,
rather blank spot in the middle of the Great Plains. Though Lewis
and Clark knew of the buffalo herds and made notations of the
same, they did not know that their "empty" spot was the heart-
land that was being fought over by the Cheyenne, Pawnee, and
Blackfeet.

Very few white trappers came through over the next decade,
and the Cheyenne may have almost forgotten about the Anglo
Americans until the summer of 1825. In that year, Brigadier General Henry Atkinson brought about 450 U.S. soldiers onto the
Northern Plains. His mission was to intimidate and to negotiate,
rather than to fight, and he persuaded a number of Plains peoples
to sign treaties with the United States. General Atkinson succeeded with the Cheyenne; High-Backed Wolf and other leading
chiefs signed the treaty on July 6, 1825. It read, in part:

> Article 1. It is admitted by the Cheyenne tribe of Indians, that
> they reside within the territorial limits of the United States,
> acknowledge their supremacy, and claim their protection—The

said tribe also admit the right of the United States to regulate all trade and intercourse with them.

This opening statement makes the modern reader wonder if the Cheyenne truly understood the words. The People had hardly heard of the United States until then, and there was no obvious, visible sign that the young American republic would eventually dominate the Plains. Chiefs such as High-Backed Wolf were not intimidated by the American Regular Army: They had never yet seen it in action. The treaty continued:

> Article 2. The United States agree to receive the Cheyenne tribe of Indians into their friendship, and under their protection, and to extend to them, from time to time, such benefits and acts of kindness as may be convenient, and seem just and proper, to the President of the United States.

John Quincy Adams was then the president—the sixth man to serve in that office. Born in far-off Massachusetts, he had little conception of the Great Plains or the many Native tribes that dwelled there. Even so, he was the first of many U.S. presidents to be called the "Great White Father" by Plains peoples.

Article 5 provided for extradition of individuals who broke the peace—on either side; it also guaranteed indemnification for any horses that might be stolen. The sixth and last article asserted that the Cheyenne would never "by sale, exchange, or as presents, supply any nation or tribe of Indians, not in amity with the United States, with guns, ammunition, or other implements of war."

General Atkinson had achieved his purpose. High-Backed Wolf and other Cheyenne chiefs felt equally positive about the treaty. To them, the Stars and Stripes—and the soldiers who marched beneath them—appeared so far off that nothing could be lost by negotiating with them. The Cheyenne leaders did not know—could not have known—that the young republic would soon send thousands—even hundreds of thousands—of settlers, eager for land in the American West.

WORST OF ENEMIES

By 1825, the Cheyenne had been on the Plains for at least two generations. They had made many friends, like the Arapaho, and some enemies, such as the Blackfeet and the Crow. Their most deadly foes, however, were the Pawnee, who lived just to the east of the Cheyenne, in what is now Kansas.

The Cheyenne and the Pawnee were both "horse people" whose lives were given to the riding of horses in the pursuit of buffalo. Both the Cheyenne and the Pawnee were renowned as horse stealers, and this may have led to their bitter enmity. By the time High-Backed Wolf and others signed the treaty with General Atkinson, they may have seen the far-off United States as a potential ally, when compared to their bitter rivalry with the Pawnee.

Historians—whether white or Native—disagree on the precise year of the great battle. It may have been in the summer of 1830, or the summer of 1832, but all sources concur that it was in the summertime that the whole Cheyenne nation picked up its tipis to go to war with the Pawnee. The two peoples had fought many times before, but this campaign represented a break with the past: The Cheyenne wanted to eliminate their foes and assume supremacy on the Northern Plains. Thanks to the writings of George Bent, whose grandfather was involved in the battle, we have some detailed knowledge of what took place, from *A Life of George Bent*:

> My grandfather called to the [young] warriors to wait, but they paid no attention. He then handed the [Sacred] Medicine Arrows to Bull who hastily tied them to the end of his lance and rode after the warriors. When he came up the Cheyennes and Sioux were in line facing the Pawnees and out between the two lines of battle a Pawnee was sitting on the ground all alone. Some say this man had been wounded, others that he had been sick a long time and was discouraged and wished to die, so he went out and sat down between the lines where he would be killed in the first charge.

The Plains region was home to several Native American groups and the Cheyenne had several enemies. Depicted in this ledger, the Cheyenne went to war with their greatest enemies, the Pawnee, in the early 1830s.

This sounds unlikely to modern ears, but Great Plains Indians often displayed what we might call a casual or fatalistic attitude toward death. Young men often charged into battle shouting that it was a good day to die. They meant that it was better to die in one's prime than to slowly wither away from weakness or disease. In this case, a Pawnee who had given up on life was about to experience one of the greatest of victories for his tribe. Bent continued:

> When Bull saw this Pawnee sitting on the ground he charged him, intending to strike him and count coup on him. As he

rushed by the man, Bull leaned over to one side and struck at him with his lance, but the Pawnee avoided the blow and grasped the lance with both hands. To avoid being pulled off his horse, Bull had to let go of the lance, and thus the lance with the great medicine of the Cheyennes tied to its point was lost.

Bull rode back to his Cheyenne line, singing a terrible mourning song. The Pawnee who now held the Sacred Arrows realized his enormous achievement and called to his Pawnee line, which surged forward. In the fierce fighting that followed, the Cheyenne managed to kill the man who had taken the arrows, but they did not recover the bundle. The Sacred Arrows—brought to The People by Sweet Medicine—were in enemy hands: the worst of all possible outcomes.

Attempts to compare this loss with others are fruitless. A U.S. Army regiment could—and sometimes did—lose its regimental colors and still fight on. A Confederate army could lose its general and continue to fight. The Sacred Arrows were something quite different, a unique blend of spiritual power intended for worldly means. Father Peter J. Powell, an Episcopal priest who spent many years with the Cheyenne, did not exaggerate when he wrote *in The Cheyennes, Maheo's People*:

> From 1830 on, two great spiritual tragedies dominate and influence the course of the People's life. The first tragedy was the most devastating. For in 1830 the Pawnees, those bitterest enemies of the Cheyennes, actually captured *Maahotse*, the Sacred Arrows, which the Creator Himself had given the tribe, and through which He pours His divine life into the People's lives.

The second tragedy, which took place in 1874, will be discussed in a later chapter.

RESTITUTION

The state of the Cheyenne in the aftermath of the battle is difficult to describe. The People were in a terrible condition, believing that they had failed Sweet Medicine and perhaps offended the Creator God. So bad was the situation that the Keeper of the Sacred Arrows (who had handed them to Bull) went to the Pawnee and practically begged for the arrows.

Bent: The Family and the Fort

Three generations of the Bent family were intimately connected with the Cheyenne, and the fort that the first generation built was one of the first seen by The People. For this reason, as well as intermarriage, the Bents of Colorado became one of the white families best known to the Cheyenne.

Born in Massachusetts in 1768, Silas Bent moved to St. Louis, Missouri (then part of the Louisiana Territory), in 1804. He had seven sons, two of whom were keenly interested in the fur trade.

William Bent (1809–1869) and Charles Bent (1799–1847) saw the potential in the moving of furs, a business that had started with French-Canadian fur trappers known as voyageurs. The Bent brothers went up the Missouri River into Sioux country in 1824 and later saw that the southern part of the Cheyenne territory was ripe for fur trade expansion. The brothers first built a stockade, and then a genuine fort, at what is now La Junta, Colorado.

Almost from their first appearance, the Bent brothers got along well with the Cheyenne, whom they had asked permission to build the fort. The brothers prospered, and William Bent raised a number of children at the fort during the time that the white settlement in southern Colorado began to grow substantially. Even though the fur trade slackened by the late 1840s, the Bent family did extremely well, as brokers for U.S. exploring groups as well as the Cheyenne. The Bents also profited by connections with Santa Fe, New Mexico.

The Pawnee did not fully comprehend the importance of the Sacred Arrows, but they saw they had the Cheyenne in a bind. An agreement was made under which one of the Sacred Arrows was returned and the others remained in Pawnee hands. In exchange,

William Bent married a Cheyenne woman, Owl Woman. The children of this marriage grew up as half-breeds, with one foot in the white person's world and the other in the tribal life of the Cheyenne. George Bent (1843–1918) married Magpie, niece of Chief Black Kettle. He began his classic autobiography with a chapter titled, "My Peoples, The Cheyennes."

Relations between the Bents and the Cheyenne remained good through the 1850s, but the beginning of the U.S. Civil War presented problems for both groups. George Bent served in the Confederate Army for a time, while his brother William was commander at Fort Bent. The Cheyenne were mystified by the conflict between the two white groups (the United States of America and the Confederate States of America), and they often turned to the Bent family for information about this conflict. Sadly, the information they received was inadequate, and the Cheyenne never made heads or tails of the great conflict that Americans call the Civil War.

Following that war, the Bent family became less influential. There were other major families in southern Colorado, and the entire area was on the road to becoming a U.S. state. To the Cheyenne, however, the name "Bent" was almost synonymous with "white merchant," and the family remained on good terms with the tribe right through the terrible battles of the 1860s and 1870s. George Bent wrote his memoirs late in life. They were lost for many years, before finally being published as *A Life of George Bent, Written from His Letters* in 1968.

the Cheyenne agreed to a lengthy peace with the Pawnee. White Thunder, the Arrow Keeper, returned home with the one arrow, and a year later the leading Cheyenne priests conducted a lengthy ceremony in which they rededicated that one and added three newly made arrows to the bundle. Some measure of balance was restored to The People, but not everyone was convinced. Some people muttered that the "replacement" arrows could never equal the potency of those that came with Sweet Medicine and that the tribe, as a whole, could expect evil times ahead.

THE WORST OF TIMES

As we saw in the opening chapter, the Cheyenne were frightened by the Night the Stars Fell, believing that they were seeing the end of the world. This fear becomes more comprehensible to us when we consider that the Leonid meteor shower came in the autumn of 1833, either one year or three years after the loss of the Sacred Arrows. Making matters worse, the Cheyenne lost one of their great leaders. High-Backed Wolf died a week or two before the night of falling stars. Given the congruence between the battle with the Pawnee, the loss of the arrows, the death of the great chief, and the night of falling stars, the Cheyenne can be forgiven for thinking they were about to enter the worst of times.

In some ways they were right.

Fort Laramie

The image of the Cheyenne that sticks in the modern mind most strongly is that of a warrior on horseback, doing battle with a blue-coated U.S. Cavalryman. There is much truth in the image—as is shown from some artistic renderings by the Cheyenne themselves—but the image is incomplete. From the time of Sweet Medicine forward, the Cheyenne labeled their greatest leaders the "peace chiefs," and The People would gladly have remained at peace with the white newcomers from the east. They did not have that opportunity.

MANIFEST DESTINY

In the mid-1840s, the term *Manifest Destiny* became common in Anglo-American circles. Echoing the remarks of a prominent New York journalist, the people who used this term meant that it was manifestly apparent that God intended for the white, Protestant,

President James K. Polk was determined to acquire more territory for the United States and managed to extend U.S. borders to the Pacific Ocean. The Cheyenne experienced the effects of Manifest Destiny when settlers began to venture west for gold and land.

Anglo-Saxon peoples to take over all of North America. As distasteful as this idea is today, one must remember that at least two-thirds of white Americans believed in it (the remaining third were either ambivalent or dead-set against it).

The election of James K. Polk as the eleventh president of the United States was a major step toward the culmination of Manifest Destiny. Born in North Carolina, Polk was an ardent believer in national expansion; his major campaign slogan had been "Fifty-Four Forty or Fight," meaning that the United States should acquire all the land up to 54 degrees and 40 minutes north latitude. While he did not achieve that grand design (the U.S.–Canadian border was drawn at the 49th parallel of north latitude), Polk managed to provoke the Republic of Mexico into a war, and in the process he won all or part of California, Colorado, New Mexico, Nevada, Utah, and Arizona. In a short year-and-a-half conflict, Polk increased the size of the United States by about 30 percent.

The Cheyenne had never looked kindly on Mexicans, and Mexico's loss in the war of 1846–1848 was of no great concern to The People until gold was discovered in California in January 1848. In the two years that followed, the Cheyenne experienced tens of thousands of U.S. migrants, passing through their lands on the way to the California gold fields. When Polk left office in March 1849, it appeared as though his vision of Manifest Destiny had practically become a reality: The Stars and Stripes extended across the continent. Many Indians were still in the way, however, and it became the task of the bluecoats (U.S. soldiers) and the gray coats (U.S. negotiators) to remove them.

HORSE CREEK (FORT LARAMIE)

President Polk was followed by President Zachary Taylor, who died in July 1850. The man who succeeded him, Vice-President Millard Fillmore, was keen to see a new Indian policy, one that would encompass all the Great Plains tribes. Neither President Fillmore nor his top advisers understood the intricacies of Great Plains diplomacy and warfare, but the men they sent west gave it their all, and if they did not succeed entirely, they certainly put on one of the greatest displays ever witnessed on the Plains. Colonel David Mitchell teamed with Indian agent Thomas Fitzpatrick;

together, they persuaded the U.S. government to send many wag-onloads of presents, which were essential to making any treaty process worthwhile. A grand council of all the Great Plains tribes was scheduled for Fort Laramie, in southeast Wyoming, on September 1, 1851.

The Cheyenne, the Pawnee, the Sioux, and the Arapaho all came. It was remarkable enough that the Cheyenne and the Pawnee would agree to share common ground, but the council also included the Shoshone (sometimes called the Snake) and the Crow, both of whom were bitter foes of many of the other tribes. By September 1, the American negotiators were present, and about 10,000 Native Americans—men, women, and children—were gathered in front of Fort Laramie. The presents had not arrived, however.

One thing that the modern reader often forgets is the absence of sanitary facilities in the nineteenth century. The large crowd of Indians, soldiers, and diplomats made the area so unsanitary that everyone moved almost 25 miles (40 kilometers) upriver to new camp sites, in present-day Nebraska. Even then, the wagon-loads of presents did not arrive, but at least the diplomats could go to work. Numerous ceremonies were conducted, including one in which the Cheyenne made amends for a recent attack on the Shoshone. Scalps were returned, and orphans were adopted by the tribe that had killed their parents. The treaty details were then hammered out:

> Article 1. The aforesaid nations, parties to this treaty, having assembled for the purposes of establishing and confirming peaceful relations amongst themselves, do hereby covenant and agree to abstain in future from all hostilities whatever against each other, to maintain good faith and friendship in all their mutual intercourse, and to make an effective and lasting peace.

Given the longstanding enmity between some of the tribes (the Cheyenne and the Pawnee especially), it was very ambitious for the U.S. government to attempt this general peace. Another key element, the U.S. diplomats said, was for the United States to have the right to establish "roads, military and other posts" in any and all of the Indian territories. None of the tribal leaders were thrilled by this idea, but all of them came around to accept it. The treaty continued:

> Article 5. The aforesaid Indian nations do hereby recognize and acknowledge the following tracts of country, including within the metes and boundaries hereinafter designated, as their respective territories. . . . The territory of the Cheyennes and Arapahoes, commencing at the Red Bute, or the place where the road leaves the north fork of the Platte River; thence up the north fork of the Platte River to its source; thence along the main range of the Rocky Mountains to the head-waters of the Arkansas River; thence down the Arkansas River to the crossing of the Santa Fe road; thence in a northwesterly direction to the forks of the Platte River, and thence up the Platte River to the place of beginning.

This delineation was not a terrible deal by any means. The major problem is that it gave the Cheyenne better, larger sections of land in their southern regions than their northern ones. The Cheyenne came off reasonably well in the treaty, and four of their leading chiefs assented to the agreement by making their marks, and thereby signing the treaty. The other tribes acted similarly, and by September 18, the day the treaty was signed, the United States and the various Great Plains tribes appeared in full accord.

The presents finally arrived two days later, and another three days were spent distributing them among the tribespeople. There were hats and officer's clothing for the leading Native American chiefs, and there were tobacco, pipes, and blankets for the more common folk. When the huge assemblage broke up, on September 25, observers accurately noted that it was the single greatest gathering ever seen on the Plains. Their predictions of a lasting peace proved much less accurate.

A Great Separation

The Cheyenne divided into their northern and southern sections sometime in the 1820s. The precise year is not known.

Until then, the Cheyenne had been one tribe, The People, powerful and indivisible. Time and circumstance combined to separate them, however, and the ramifications would be long lasting.

Part of the reason lay with the tribe's great success. In the 1810s and 1820s, the Cheyenne made great headway against their traditional foes (Pawnee, Blackfeet, and others), expanding the size of the Cheyenne tribal lands. Instead of being largely in what are now Wyoming and South Dakota, the Cheyenne had new territories in what are now Colorado and Kansas. There was even a tribal movement—however small—in the direction of what are now Arizona and New Mexico.

During the time that High-Backed Wolf led the Cheyenne, The People divided into the northern and southern sections. The Cheyenne did not expect this separation to be permanent, and—had there been no influx of Anglo Americans—there might have been a complete tribal reorganization sometime later. The Cheyenne success, and their subsequent breaking into two groups, however, rendered them vulnerable to encroachment by white settlers, fur traders, and the like.

The division between Northern and Southern Cheyenne remains today. Most of The People will readily say that they are one nation, one blood, and there is much visitation between the northern and southern groups, but almost two centuries of living in different habitats have made the Northern and Southern Cheyenne fairly different. Two things that hold them together, that make them continue to think in terms of "one" are the Sacred Buffalo Hat (now in residence in Montana) and the Sacred Arrows (now in residence in Oklahoma).

SHOT HEARD OVER THE PLAINS

Those familiar with the start of the American Revolution know that we remain ignorant about who fired the first musket ball, the "shot heard round the world." In the case of the evening skirmish that ignited a long series of wars on the Plains, we know who fired the first shot, but there are discrepancies in the record about how it happened.

The Treaty of Fort Laramie was intended to last forever, but the increasing number of white immigrants on the Plains made this impossible. As more and more whites (headed for California and Oregon) passed through Indian country, the separation between tribes—including the Northern and Southern Cheyenne—became worse. Just as bad, the immigrants killed or chased off so many buffalo that the Plains tribes were reduced to beggary and want. Compounding the troubles were the quality of the Anglo-American soldiers stationed at the handful of forts. Bored by peacetime, wishing to make names for themselves, and generally contemptuous of Native American fighting qualities, these young men were almost bound to raise conflicts with the Indians.

On August 18, 1854—three years after the signing of the treaty—a Mormon immigrant group was passing through Sioux country on its way to Fort Laramie. A cow broke free from the group and wandered into a nearby Sioux camp, where it was killed and eaten. According to general custom on the Plains, this action was acceptable and should, at most, have been answered with a money settlement. The Anglo-American commander at Fort Laramie thought differently, however, and he sent Second Lieutenant John L. Grattan to apprehend the man who had stolen the cow. At that moment, there were no cavalry units at Fort Laramie, so Lieutenant Grattan set out with 38 men and two howitzers (small cannon). The Sioux and Cheyenne (it was a mixed camp) could easily have ridden away, but they allowed the Anglo-American force to approach. In his history of Fort Laramie, Remi Nadeau describes what happened at the Sioux camp on the evening of August 19, 1854:

Lucien [an interpreter] spoke to Grattan—possibly giving an interpretation of Man-Afraid's words. "How! How!" Grattan answered, using the Indian term for "I understand and agree." Immediately one of the soldiers stepped forward and aimed his musket at the Indians standing in front. Possibly he had understood Grattan to say, "Now! Now!" He fired, and one of the Indians fell.

Much like the evening of March 5, 1770, when seven British soldiers fired into a group of Bostonians in front of that town's Customs House, accounts differ as to the words used and commands issued. Quite possibly, Lieutenant Grattan did not order his men to fire, but one of them heard something that made him act, and within minutes, the standoff in front of the Sioux tents had turned into a bloodbath.

Lieutenant Grattan and nearly all his men died that night. The Sioux and Cheyenne were so angry that they speared the dead men's bodies, making some of them unrecognizable. That opening rifle shot—fired by a soldier who misunderstood his commander—set the Great Plains afire.

RETRIBUTION

News got around faster than before, because of the recent advent of the telegraph. U.S. military leaders learned of the violence in and around Fort Laramie, and President Franklin Pierce decided on strong action against the Sioux and their Cheyenne allies.

Brigadier General William S. Harney was selected to lead an expedition to the Plains. Born in Tennessee in 1800, Harney had been a young man of 25 when he accompanied Brigadier General Henry Atkinson on the expedition that culminated in the signing of the first treaties between the United States and the various Plains tribes. Now 55, Harney had a formidable reputation as an Indian fighter, gained from expeditions against the Black Hawk tribe in 1832 and the Seminole in 1840.

Harney brought almost 1,000 Regular Army troops to bear on the Sioux, whom he defeated in the Battle of Ash Hollow, in Kansas, in September 1855. His chastisement of the Sioux was followed by Colonel E.V. Sumner's defeat of the Cheyenne on the Republican River in Colorado in 1857. These two engagements demonstrated the numerical superiority of the U.S. troops. There were far more bluecoats than Indian warriors, and the American soldiers had—when viewed from Indian eyes—the uncanny ability to stay in the field as long as it took to obtain a victory. By contrast, many Plains tribes believed in short campaigns—seldom more than a month—and in inflicting casualties on the enemy without trying to eliminate them. Some Plains people found it appalling that the U.S. Army employed no system of "honor" in war. There was no honor in counting coup, for example, only the brutal satisfaction of killing a foe.

WARRIOR SOCIETIES

Even after the punishment inflicted on the Republican River, the Cheyenne did not fully understand the size and strength of the U.S. military. The few Cheyenne who had ever gone east to visit the "Great White Father" were ridiculed when they returned with stories of railroads, military encampments, and great cities. How could the Great Father ever feed or clothe so many people, the listeners asked?

The Cheyenne had long had their four major warrior societies, but in the years that followed the first battles with the bluecoats, the Dog Soldiers became more important than before. Unlike the Fox Society, or the Elk group, the Dog Soldiers generally believed in unrelenting warfare on the white peoples who continued to pass through Cheyenne country in ever-increasing numbers. Not everyone agreed with the Dog Soldiers; a separation of beliefs began to emerge within The People during the late 1850s. There were those who believed that peace with the whites was a necessity, and in the winter of 1863, a group of Plains leaders—including

In 1863, a delegation of Plains leaders went to Washington, D.C., to address their concerns about westward expansion with President Abraham Lincoln. Above, the delegation and Mary Todd Lincoln (*far right*) visit the White House Conservatory.

several Cheyenne—traveled to Washington, D.C., to meet the Great Father and tell him their troubles. In his biography of Chief Black Kettle, author Thom Hatch describes the meeting of the delegation of Cheyenne, Arapaho, Caddo, Comanche, and Kiowa leaders with President Abraham Lincoln at the White House:

> Lincoln responded to the chiefs by saying that although the whites were engaged in a war against each other, they were not a warring race that wished to fight the red man. He told the chiefs that the whites were strong and prosperous because they depended on farming, rather than on hunting, for subsistence and added, "I really am not capable of advising you whether, in

the providence of the Great Spirit, who is the Great Father of us all, it is for you to maintain the habits and customs of your race, or to adopt a new mode of life. I can only say that I can see no way in which your race is to become as prosperous as the white race, except by living as they do, by cultivation of the earth."

Each chief was given an American flag, the flag of the Union rather than the Confederacy. Each chief believed that flying this flag was a symbol of his friendship with President Lincoln, the Great Father in Washington, D.C. All of the chiefs who were in Washington that day, in March 1863, would be disappointed, but Chief Black Kettle would be the most disappointed of all.

Massacres and Migrations

The Civil War—between the 20 states of the Union and the 11 states of the Confederacy—began in April 1861. The War Between the States, as it was called, does not figure largely in Cheyenne tribal history, but The People soon realized that their position, on the "hinge" of the western frontier, made it impossible for them to ignore this quarrel between the Anglo Americans.

BENT FAMILY

Even the Bent family, which had lived so successfully on the edge of the white and Indian worlds, was torn by the War Between the States. George Bent (1843–1918) described the tensions in southern Colorado and northern New Mexico:

> [One] story was that the Confederates were plotting with the Indians and preparing for a combined attack on the frontier settlements and the overland roads. This rumor was about half

true, as the Confederates were really planning an attack on the Arkansas River posts. In the summer of 1861, Captain Albert Pike, the author of the version of Dixie which was sung in the South during the war, was sent by the Richmond government to attempt to gain over the tribes in Indian Territory [present-day Oklahoma].

The Confederate States of America (CSA) was quicker than the Union (USA) to see that Colorado and New Mexico were key to winning the West. Once the Union realized the danger, however, it had more resources to hold on to that area. Like most other Plains Indians, the Cheyenne were confused by the Civil War, which they saw as a family quarrel between the white peoples.

By 1863, the year that several Cheyenne chiefs met President Abraham Lincoln, the Cheyenne were decidedly separated into their northern and southern components. This was not a desire on the part of The People; rather, the situation had been forced upon them. It meant that they were divided at a time when the Cheyenne most needed tribal unity and that no side could truly claim to represent all 44 council chiefs. Into this dangerous situation stepped Black Kettle, whom author Thom Hatch has labeled the "chief who sought peace but found war."

BLACK KETTLE

Born sometime between 1800 and 1812 (accounts vary), Black Kettle grew up when the Cheyenne were still the number-one presence on the Northern Plains. During the 1840s and 1850s, he saw the tribal lands shrink—due to treaties and ongoing conflicts with other tribes—and by the time he met President Lincoln in the White House, Black Kettle was convinced that the Cheyenne had to make peace with these powerful white people from the east. Simply put, there were too many U.S. soldiers to fight.

By mid-1864, with the Civil War still raging, the Cheyenne were aware that even their beloved homeland in Colorado was imperiled. Thousands of white settlers had come west in 1859, after silver was discovered in the Colorado mountains, and the towns of Leadville and Denver had been established. Black Kettle was old enough to remember when there were no white people in Colorado, and he may even have been present when a handful of Cheyenne chiefs allowed William Bent to build his first fort, in present-day La Junta, Colorado. Black Kettle had to put nostalgia aside. He knew that the Cheyenne were too few to stop the Anglo-American settlers, and he was even willing to entertain the idea of settling down as a farmer. Not all of The People agreed with him, however.

DOG SOLDIERS

The winter of 1863–1864 was especially hard for the Cheyenne. The buffalo herds of previous years were much diminished, and many of The People did not have enough to eat. When they learned, in the spring of 1864, that the Northern Cheyenne were organizing a campaign against the Crow Indians, many Dog Soldiers among the Southern Cheyenne decided to go. On their way north, the Dog Soldiers ran into a series of cattlemen and soldier groups, and the skirmishes that took place set off the Cheyenne War of 1864. Though they had left home intending to strike a blow at a Native foe, the Dog Soldiers rekindled war between the Cheyenne and their more-numerous white neighbors.

Black Kettle saw his role as that of a peace chief, not a war leader. On more than one occasion, he rode between Cheyenne and white lines, persuading both sides to back off. Valiant as his efforts were, they were insufficient to prevent deep mistrust between the Southern Cheyenne and the white settlers of Colorado, who feared an all-out Indian war. The example of the Santee Sioux, in 1862, was very much on their minds.

THE GOVERNOR AND THE COLONEL

John Evans arrived in Denver in May 1862 as the new territorial governor of Colorado. A physician and a real-estate speculator,

Santee Sioux Uprising

Normally one associates Abraham Lincoln with the Civil War, the great struggle between the Union and the Confederacy. Lincoln's presidency was also occupied with western troubles, though, and none of them loomed larger than the Santee Sioux uprising in the spring of 1862.

Misunderstandings between Sioux leaders and American commissioners were compounded by a harsh winter, which left many of the Sioux hungry. A series of small fights escalated into a major revolt, with hundreds, perhaps thousands of Sioux on the warpath. The U.S. government was surprised, because Minnesota had been free of Indian conflict for many years. Once the government learned the magnitude of the revolt, however, thousands of soldiers were sent, and when all was said and done, about 800 whites and a far greater number of Sioux were killed.

Hundreds of Sioux were put in military prison, and after a series of hasty trials, about 303 of them were sentenced to death. To his credit, President Lincoln required that the records be sent to him in Washington, where he personally reviewed each case. When he was finished, the president announced that only about 38 of the 303 would be hanged. This was clemency, and Lincoln at his best, but there is no way to gloss over the fact that his presidency witnessed some of the most extreme fighting between Indians and Anglo Americans.

Evans had already experienced much success in life (Evanston, Illinois, is named for him). Evans had many fine qualities, but understanding Native Americans—whether Sioux or Cheyenne— was not among them. Soon after coming to Denver, Evans became alarmed that the Santee Sioux uprising was about to be repeated in Colorado, and he made repeated requests to Washington, D.C., asking for more infantry and cavalry to defend the territory. Some of his requests were honored, but every time there was a scare in the overall Civil War, troops were yanked from Colorado and sent back east. Governor Evans decided he needed something more reliable, and he turned to Colonel John Chivington to supply a local militia force.

Born in Ohio in 1821, Chivington was an ordained Methodist minister with a violent streak. Arriving in Colorado in 1860, Chivington made a name for himself, both as a fine preacher and as a military leader. He recruited a volunteer unit known as the Fighting Sixth and was prepared for action against any foes: Confederates, desperadoes, or Indians. The Cheyenne Indian War of 1864 gave him a perfect opportunity.

On June 27, 1864, Governor Evans sent a letter addressed to all the "Friendly Indians of the Plains." Noting that livestock had been stolen and that skirmishes had been fought, Governor Evans ordered the friendly Cheyenne and Arapaho to go to Fort Lyon (previously Bent's Fort), where they would receive provisions and safety from the fort commander. Any Indians who did not repair to a fort, or report to an Anglo-American commander, would be considered hostiles. Governor Evans ended his letter with the warning that "the war on hostile Indians will be continued until they are all effectually subdued," as quoted in Thom Hatch's biography of Black Kettle.

At issue was whether the Southern Cheyenne were to become a true "reservation" tribe or whether they would continue to lead the free life of their ancestors. Black Kettle led his Southern Cheyenne, and a small group of Arapaho, to Sand Creek, near Fort Lyon. The chief was obeying the letter of the law, as laid down by Governor Evans, but some U.S. military leaders believed he had already betrayed its spirit. Black Kettle simply wanted to wait out the winter in safety, they said, to resume the conflict in the spring of 1865. Everything that is known of Black Kettle suggests this is

Even though Chief Black Kettle holds the U.S. flag, a Colorado militia-man attacks him anyway. This is one reason the Sand Creek Massacre is known as one of the worst offenses of the Plains Indian Wars.

not the case, but he did not speak for all the Cheyenne, and provo-cations had been offered from both sides.

Black Kettle and his group of about 400 Cheyenne and Arap-aho had experienced the first, early blasts of winter, but they were not prepared for something much worse: an attack by the Denver militia. As author Thom Hatch describes it in *Black Kettle*, "A group of determined men, led by a Methodist minister turned diabolical militia commander, was riding toward a rendezvous with infamy."

SAND CREEK MASSACRE

Colonel Chivington brought his Denver militia out at the end of November 1864. Not only was Chivington convinced that the Cheyenne were intractable hostiles who needed to be chastised, but he had persuaded his men, too. How Chivington managed to square this with the simple fact that Black Kettle and his band were living quietly, under the protection of the garrison at Fort Lyon, is unknown. The simple, painful facts are that Chivington and his men

- arrived on the morning of November 29, and fired cannon shots into the camp;
- charged across the river, and attacked men, women, and children, many of whom were just waking from sleep;
- killed as many as 150 Cheyenne, and brutally savaged the bodies of many of the fallen.

Black Kettle hoisted his American flag, but found it was no use. Finding his wife, who had been hit by no fewer than nine bullets, he made it to a section farther up the river, where he and some of his men held the Anglo-American attack off long enough to organize a retreat. Black Kettle and Medicine Lodge (his wife) made it to safety.

Those who have studied the Sand Creek Massacre eventually come to the conclusion that it is one of the most disgraceful actions ever taken under the U.S. flag. Militiamen, mustered for the purpose of keeping the peace, savagely attacked and destroyed a Native American encampment, offering neither quarter nor honor for the fallen. If Sand Creek had happened at an earlier time, say in 1854, or at a later one such as 1874, it might have earned greater denunciation. As it was, coming when the Civil War was approaching its bloody climax, Sand Creek was seen as merely another regrettable lapse in humanity.

WAR'S END

The Civil War ended in April 1865, with the surrender of the Army of Northern Virginia at Appomattox Court House, Virginia. By that time, the Union armies had reached a staggering total of about 300,000 men under arms, and if just one-tenth of that number had been sent west, there might have been no future U.S.–Indian wars, thanks to such a show of force. The North rapidly demobilized after 1865, however, and the western garrisons of 1866 and 1867 were only slightly larger than those of 1863 and 1864. Possibly, this led to a renewal of American-Cheyenne conflict.

The Dog Soldiers remained the most militant of all the Cheyenne. Incensed by the Sand Creek Massacre, they organized a series of attacks on Anglo-American settlements and wagon trains. What most disturbed the Dog Soldiers was the talk of a railroad to be run through their country; what most disturbed the Anglo-American settlers of Kansas and Colorado was the idea that the Dog Soldiers would resist such a move. By 1867—when the planned Transcontinental Railroad was in the process of being built—a second U.S.–Cheyenne war broke out. Like that of 1864, it was not "declared" by either side; instead, it developed from a series of aggressions and counteraggressions.

In the spring of 1867, General Philip Sheridan had overall command of the U.S. forces on the Great Plains. A highly accomplished Civil War cavalry commander, Sheridan had on his staff the most celebrated of all U.S. Cavalrymen: George Armstrong Custer. Only 27 when he first came to the Great Plains, Custer was famous for his daring Civil War actions; even his detractors admitted he was a terrific horseman and motivator of men. Compared with the Battles of Gettysburg and The Wilderness, which had involved almost 100,000 men on each side, the Great Plains Indian wars seemed like small stuff, but Brigadier General Custer saw the making of his fame. As soon as he took command of the Seventh Cavalry, Custer had his men "color" their mounts, so they would be recognizable from a distance. He was a terrific battlefield commander, but he was also a highly skilled public-relations operator.

WINTER CAMPAIGN

Custer overreached himself in 1867 and was court-martialed for disobeying orders. He had to surrender his rank for a full year, but

After surviving the Sand Creek Massacre, Black Kettle traveled with a group of Cheyenne that were attacked near the Washita River. Led by Brigadier General George Armstrong Custer, the 7th Cavalry massacred the band of Cheyenne and scalped Black Kettle.

when he came back to the field, in the autumn of 1868, circumstances conspired to give him greater opportunities than before. It was an example of what he called "Custer's Luck."

General William T. Sherman—who had led the devastating Union march from Atlanta to the sea in 1864—was convinced that the Plains Indians could not be defeated by conventional means. Their horses were swifter than those of the U.S. Cavalry, and they dispersed at the most unlikely times, leaving hardly a trace. The only way to strike these foes, Sherman decided, was to mount a winter campaign and find their most hidden villages at the time of year when The People were most vulnerable. The difficulty, as some critics pointed out, was that the U.S. Cavalry would be equally vulnerable: Temperatures on the Plains sometimes dipped to -40°F (-40°C). No previous U.S. Army action (not even the winter of Valley Forge or the Christmas Surprise at Trenton) had been carried out under such circumstances. General Sherman turned to General Sheridan, who practically begged General Custer to return to the field.

MASSACRE ON THE WASHITA

Custer took up command of the Seventh Cavalry in October 1868. He showed his usual dash and skill, turning his hard-bitten men into winter fighters. By the middle of November, his scouts had picked up a Cheyenne trail that led deep into the heart of Indian country: present-day Oklahoma.

Custer motivated his men through personal example. He drove them through November 1868, and on November 26, the day before Thanksgiving, his scouts found a large Cheyenne village, or group of lodges. Custer had no way of knowing that this was Black Kettle's band. The Cheyenne chief had survived the Sand Creek Massacre, but he would not be as lucky on the Washita.

Custer attacked at dawn on November 27. In *The Battle of the Washita*, historian Stan Hoig describes the opening of the attack:

> Custer, riding a black stallion and accompanied by his scouts and staff, led the charge down the steep bank of the Washita, clearing the trail crossing of the Washita at a single jump. Inside the village area, he encountered a Cheyenne warrior, who jerked up his rifle to draw a bead on the cavalryman. But, according to his own claim, Custer quickly proved the value of past battle experience and his accuracy with a pistol. He shot the Indian through the head before he could get off a shot.

Within five minutes, Black Kettle's village became the scene of a grisly melee. Troopers galloped hither and fro, alternately using their carbines and swords. Cheyenne men—old and young— mounted their best resistance, occasionally knocking off a U.S. Cavalryman, but the attack was so swift and sudden that their efforts were hopeless. Black Kettle and his wife escaped to the Washita and were halfway across it before they were felled by bullets (U.S. troopers later displayed the peace chief's scalp). A small band of Cheyenne found a pit in which to mount a defense. They took a serious toll on Custer's cavalry before being overwhelmed. One of the few eyewitness accounts is from the Cheyenne woman Moving Behind, whose words were recorded many years later in *The Battle of the Washita*:

> In this grass we lay flat, our hearts beating fast; and we were afraid to move. It was now broad daylight. It frightened us to listen to the noise and the cries of the wounded. When the noise seemed to quiet down, and we believed the battle was about to end, we raised our heads high enough to see what was going on. We saw a dark figure lying near a hill, and later we learned it was the body of a [Cheyenne] woman with child. The woman's body had been cut open by the soldiers.

Custer's men counted 103 dead warriors. Fifty-three Cheyenne—almost all women and children—were taken prisoner. Almost as important was the loss of matériel. Custer counted 241 saddles, 573 buffalo robes, 360 untanned robes, 35 revolvers, 47 rifles, and 250 pounds of lead as the spoils of war. He torched the village, destroying all the lodges but one.

To many Americans in 1868, Custer was the war hero *par excellence.* To some of his superiors, he was a man of great skill, and an even greater ego that often got him into trouble. To The People, however, Custer was the worst of all American foes, an enemy who aimed at nothing less than the destruction of their way of life.

Custer and
Little Bighorn

The majority of stories connected to George A. Custer and the Little Bighorn come from Anglo-American sources. Thankfully, a handful of dedicated scholars have amassed a collection of Native American memories of the event.

GRANT'S PRESIDENCY

Ulysses S. Grant, the victorious Union general, won election to the White House in November 1868. The news of Custer's "victory" or "massacre" at Washita came to Washington, D.C., just weeks later. Some Americans were elated, thinking that the Plains Indian Wars were over, but others were skeptical of Custer's claims that a general peace was possible with all the Indians on the Plains. President Grant appointed Indian commissioners and specifically announced that members of the Society of Friends (Quakers) were his first choice to fill the posts.

Grant's sincere desire for peace was blunted by events, how-ever. In November 1873, the United States experienced the start of a severe economic depression. The Panic of 1873 began on Wall Street and spread to most corners of American life. When the aver-age citizen learned that there was a way out (however specious), he or she was eager to take advantage. The way out of the Panic of 1873 appeared to be the discovery of gold in the Black Hills of the Dakota Territory. That area was sacred to the Lakota Sioux, the Cheyenne, and several others Plains tribes.

CUSTER IN THE HILLS

In the summer of 1874, General Custer went west, this time to lead an expedition to the Black Hills. Few Anglo Americans had ever been inside the Black Hills, and fewer still understood how sacred they were to a number of tribes. What Custer's expedition did discover was that there was indeed gold in the hills, and, over time, a particular section would yield about $2 billion worth of the yellow dust.

To the Cheyenne, what mattered was that Custer had invaded the sacred hills, very close to Noahvose (Sacred or Holy Moun-tain). The Northern Cheyenne had long been friendly with the Teton (Western) Sioux. The two peoples now made a firm pact to resist any effort by the Anglo Americans to take over the Black Hills. Thousands of white miners descended on the Black Hills. The Sioux and Northern Cheyenne tried to keep the peace, but it proved impossible, and the U.S. government provided the final straw, ordering all Northern Plains Indians to report to agencies (reservations) by January 1, 1876. Those who failed to do so would be considered hostile.

Around the same time (the precise date is uncertain), the Northern Cheyenne experienced a loss nearly equal to the terrible day in 1830, when the Skidi Pawnee captured the Sacred Arrows. The Sacred Buffalo Hat, which had come down from Erect Horns, had been safely kept by one man after another, for generations, but in 1874, The People learned that the wife of its Keeper—hearing that her husband was about to be displaced as Keeper—ripped one of the horns from the buffalo hat. She made off with it, a theft that was discovered weeks later when a sacred ceremony was held.

Brigadier General George Custer is one of the most complex personalities of U.S. military history. At once admired, feared, and loathed, he was the driving force behind the massacre at the Washita River in 1868 and then led the 7th Cavalry to disaster at the Battle of Little Bighorn.

Though the new Keeper of the Sacred Hat was able to repair the physical damage, the psychological damage was immense. *Is'siwun*, the sacred cap, had been violated, and The People expected evil tidings in the immediate future.

SITTING BULL AND PRESIDENT GRANT

The renowned Sioux chief Sitting Bull is justly remembered for his valiant stands against the Anglo Americans. So much attention has been paid to him, however, that many of today's readers do not realize that the Sioux *and* the Northern Cheyenne jointly carried out the resistance to the white invasion of the Black Hills. Both peoples were imperiled by the settlement and the appearance of the gold miners.

By the early spring of 1876, Sitting Bull and Crazy Horse—the two leading Sioux chiefs—had gathered about 2,000 warriors (Sioux and Northern Cheyenne) near the border of present-day Montana and North Dakota. The Indians knew that the U.S. government was sending a force against them; how large that force was remained unknown.

Grant was in his last year as president of the United States. Not only was his tenure fast disappearing, but he was keenly aware that 1876 was the centennial year, in which Americans would celebrate the 100th anniversary of the signing of the Declaration of Independence. Even as he prepared to lead the centennial ceremonies in Philadelphia, President Grant issued orders for General Alfred Terry, General George Crook, and General George Custer to crush the Sioux and Northern Cheyenne. As usual, the U.S. Cavalry was the most important instrument, and Custer was the most celebrated war leader. Even though he was second in command to General Terry, Custer was the best-known leader of the three-pronged expedition.

The U.S. forces mustered in the early spring and converged on the Yellowstone and Missouri rivers by June.

CHEYENNE ACCOUNTS

Even as late as 1876—when they had been at war with the United States for a decade—the Northern Cheyenne still considered counting coup the most important aspect of a battle. This meant touching an enemy with a lance, a riding crop, or even a stick. Counting coup had been central to the Cheyenne way of war for generations. Scalping was certainly in their repertoire, but the Cheyenne most honored the man who counted coup on the enemy, showing his courage and skill.

By contrast, the U.S. Cavalry had developed a kill-or-be-killed attitude toward most of the Plains Indians. No one ever recorded the actual speech, but it was said that General William T. Sherman claimed that the only good Indian was a dead one. In head-on clashes, this disparity of sentiment put the Indians at a disadvantage. *They* might be satisfied with counting coup on the enemy, but *he* was out to kill them.

John Stands in Timber related the first battle that June between the Northern Cheyenne and the U.S. troopers:

> The warriors behind them [the scouts] were getting ready for battle. Many had ceremonies to perform and ornaments to put on before they went into war, and they knew it would not be long. So the chiefs gave the order and the warriors howled like wolves to answer them, and scattered here and there to begin picking out their shields and warbonnets and other things they used. Not too many had warbonnets, though. More used mounted birds or animals and had different kinds of charms.

The Northern Cheyenne had developed a distinctive attitude toward war. Counting coup was the greatest glory that an individual could attain, but there was also a suicidal urge that took over some of the young men. Some swore suicide oaths, vowing never to return from the battle alive. Other, generally older men helped them get ready.

In Anglo-American history, the fight of June 17, 1876, is known as Crook's Fight on the Rosebud River, but the Northern Cheyenne call it "Where the Girl Saved Her Brother." The two opposing forces had scouted and reconnoitered for days before coming to grips in the heat of June 17 (the summer of 1876 was especially warm). The battle itself was a long skirmish, with much galloping back and forth, and thousands of bullets fired, but few casualties. For the Northern Cheyenne, the key moment—the one they remember best—was when Chief Comes in Sight had his horse shot from under him. He was halfway between the white and Indian forces and was probably shouting what he believed would be his last defiant war cry, when, according to *Cheyenne Memories*:

> His sister had ridden with the warriors that day. She was watch-ing him and she saw the soldier scouts start down to kill him. She came on the run as soon as his horse somersaulted over, and Comes in Sight jumped on behind her and they got away. The Cheyennes named the battle for that.

The clash on the Rosebud was indecisive, but it held General Crook back for days. During that time, General Custer made one of his typically valiant moves. On this occasion, valiance led to foolhardiness. One reason the Northern Cheyenne and the Sioux respected and remembered Custer so well was that he acted like them. Just as they galloped into battle shouting that it was a good day to die, Custer showed no fear.

LITTLE BIGHORN

June 25, 1876, is one of the red-letter dates of American history. Almost all schoolchildren know that Custer fought the Sioux and that he and his men perished in what has been called Custer's Last Stand. Like many great moments from history, the Last Stand is interpreted and then reinterpreted by each new generation. One of the most recent accounts, drawing on both white and Native sources, is Nathaniel Philbrick's *The Last Stand*. The following account uses both Philbrick's book and the words of John Stands in Timber, published in 1967. Stands in Timber described the morning of June 25:

> The Indians held a parade for the boys who had been in the sui-cide dance the night before. . . . It was customary to put on such

Custer's exploration of the Black Hills angered the Cheyenne and the Sioux, and the two tribes collaborated in an attack against Custer's forces in 1876. The Battle of the Little Bighorn was an undisputed victory for the Native Americans. The event, depicted above, became known as Custer's Last Stand.

a parade after a suicide dance. The boys went in front, with an old man on either side announcing to the public to look at these boys well; they would never come back after the next battle. They paraded down through the Cheyenne camp on the inside and back on the outside.

Those who had pledged to fight to the death were boys, but there was also a group of young men who had vowed to count coup or die. They were the first to spot Custer and his men, who came galloping toward the village early in the afternoon. Though his Crow scouts told him that the Sioux and Cheyenne were very numerous, Custer showed no fear. His only concern was that the foe would get away.

Indian Women and Custer

Considering that George A. Custer was the greatest foe of their people, Cheyenne women appear to have taken an unusually appreciative view of "Long Hair," as Custer was known. Perhaps this is because he embodied the type of fearlessness that was admired in Cheyenne men, the idea that "this is a good day to die."

In 1928, Kate Bighead, a Northern Cheyenne woman, related her story to Thomas B. Marquis, an Anglo-American physician who had come to live with The People. She knew no English, so they communicated in sign language. Marquis, who also took many well-known photographs of The People, was a careful listener, and he was able to take down her words concerning Custer and the Battle of the Little Bighorn. As cited in *The Custer Reader*, she said:

> [Custer] had a large nose, deep-set eyes, and light-red hair that was long and wavy. He was wearing a buckskin suit and a big white hat. I was then a young woman, 22 years old, and I admired him. All of the Indian women talked of him as being a fine-looking man.

Kate Bighead had been at the Battle (Massacre) of the Washita in 1868. By odd chance, she was also at the Northern Cheyenne village on June 25, 1876, when Custer and his men attacked. Her account continues:

On a bluff just outside the camp, Custer and his men paused for 20 minutes. Neither the white nor the Indian accounts are able to show exactly why, but the Cheyenne developed a humorous description of the event. Knowing of Custer's great liking for women, they put these words into his mouth, "When

We heard shooting. We hid in the brush. The sounds of the shooting multiplied—pop-pop-pop-pop! We heard women and children screaming. Old men were calling the young warriors to battle. Young men were singing their war songs as they responded to the call.

Kate Bighead and her companions remained in safety for as long as they could. When they emerged, they saw the middle and end parts of the battle. According to Bighead, a number of the U.S. soldiers went crazy, shooting themselves in the head rather than surrendering. Hers is one of several Native testimonies to that effect, and archaeologists have long attempted to understand the battle scene better, through the use of her words.

Bighead is also one of the few sources that delineates Custer's relationship with a Cheyenne woman. Her cousin Me-o-tzi met Custer in the spring of 1869, months after the Battle of the Washita, and, according to Bighead, the two had a passionate relationship. Her cousin was so distressed upon learning of Custer's death that she "cut off her hair and gashed her arms and legs in mourning."

The full truth of Custer's fondness for Native American women—and their admiration for him—is unlikely ever to be known. For the twenty-first century reader, however, the attachment between friend and foe, white man and Native woman is a telling example of how attraction can transcend the lines of ethnicity.

we get to that village I'm going to find the Sioux girl with the most elk teeth on her dress and take her along with me." If these words are accurate, then Custer may have been looking for a girl just like She-Who-Bathes-Her-Knees, described in the opening chapter.

Resuming the attack, Custer charged over the river and into the village. The suicide boys leaped from trees onto the soldiers' mounts, throwing some of them off, and commencing the battle proper. None of the suicide boys survived, but all of their names are remembered today. As the fighting grew more vicious, the white soldiers were pinned into a small area where Custer made his last stand. John Stands in Timber attempted to answer one of the key questions:

> Everyone always wants to know who killed Custer. I have inter-
> preted twice for people asking about this, and whether anyone
> ever saw a certain Indian take a shot and kill him. But they
> always denied it. Too many people were shooting. Nobody
> could tell whose bullet killed a certain man. There were rumors
> some knew but would not say anything for fear of trouble. But
> it was more like Spotted Blackbird said: "If we could have seen
> where each bullet landed, we might have known. But hundreds
> of bullets were flying that day."

Perhaps around three in the afternoon, it all was over. Custer and his men lay dead on the ground that the Indians call the Greasy Grass. The Sioux and Northern Cheyenne held a victory dance that night, at which the suicide boys were especially honored. The twin tribes had won a spectacular victory over "Yellow Hair," the American they feared *and* admired the most. They had little idea, though, of what their victory would eventually mean.

REACTION AND RESPONSE

There were no survivors on the white side. Major Marcus Reno and his detachment learned by finding the dead bodies. Even though Reno sent word posthaste, it was a long way to the nearest telegraph office, and not until July 7, three days after the celebration of the centennial, did Americans learn of Custer's Last Stand and ultimate defeat.

Readers in the twenty-first century have little sense of how nineteenth-century Americans viewed the Plains Indians. Rather

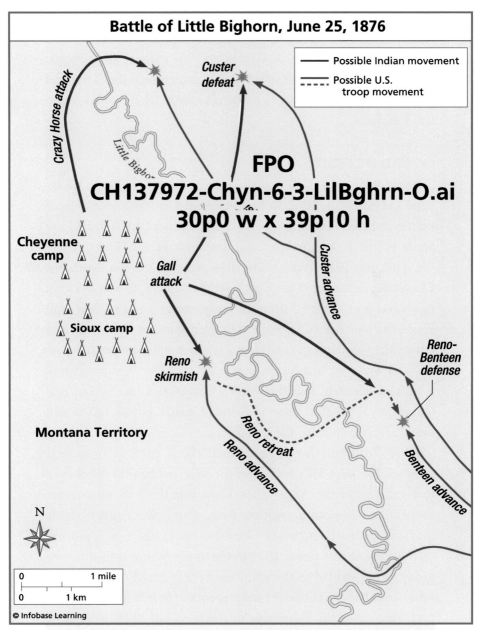

Battle of Little Bighorn, June 25, 1876

—— Possible Indian movement

----- Possible U.S. troop movement

Crazy Horse attack

Little Bigho

Custer defeat

FPO
CH137972-Chyn-6-3-LilBghrn-O.ai
30p0 w x 39p10 h

Cheyenne camp

Gall attack

Custer advance

Sioux camp

Reno skirmish

Reno-Benteen defense

Montana Territory

Reno retreat

Reno advance

Benteen advance

N

0   1 mile
0   1 km

© Infobase Learning

Custer's entire cavalry troop was killed when they attacked Cheyenne and Sioux at the Little Bighorn River. The victory was the last for Indians in the West. This map shows possible troop and Indian movements in the battle.

than singing the praises of a warrior people making a valiant attempt to preserve their way of life, Americans of 1876 declared the need for vengeance. If Custer and his men of the Seventh Cavalry were dead, then the U.S. Army must sweep the Sioux and Northern Cheyenne from the Plains entirely. There could be no half measures.

TOTAL DEFEAT

The winter of 1876–1877 was calamitous for the Northern Cheyenne and the Sioux. The U.S. Army came at them with greater force than ever before. In September 1876, the Americans defeated the Sioux at Slim Buttes, which the Indians named the "Fight Where We Lost the Black Hills." The troopers chased the Northern Cheyenne, defeating them on November 25, 1876, and drawing the noose ever tighter during the early winter. Led by Chief Dull Knife, the Northern Cheyenne struggled through the winter and joined the Oglala Sioux in February. Their situation was desperate, and when leading Sioux, such as Crazy Horse, surrendered, it became apparent that their defeat was total. Chief Sitting Bull had escaped over the border to British Canada, but he, too, would eventually surrender to the U.S. forces.

The Northern Cheyenne council chiefs debated their next move. Some were for continuing the fight, while others believed that yielding to the Anglo Americans was the only alternative. Rather than impose a solution from above, the council chiefs declared that each and every Cheyenne could make up his or her own mind. At this point, the Northern Cheyenne split into two groups. One yielded to the white soldiers at Fort Keogh, and the other went back to the reservation agency at White River. The former were especially vulnerable to the persuasions of the American leaders, notably General Nelson A. Miles, who had won the battles over the winter. Miles urged the Northern Cheyenne to make a great journey south, to join their kinsmen in the Indian Territory, which is now Oklahoma. Accounts of the discussions vary, but almost all the Native ones claim that General Miles said the Northern Cheyenne could move on a provisional basis, that they could return north if they disliked the south. The main body of Cheyenne asked Chief Standing Elk to deliver their answer to General Miles. They believed he would reject Miles's offer, but Standing Elk declared that he—and most of the Cheyenne—were ready to make the move to join their southern brethren.

The great move began in the summer of 1877.

Exodus

In the long history of the Cheyenne, no single event stands out as clearly as the exodus from Oklahoma in 1878. Anglo-American historians and novelists have been as entranced by the story as their Native counterparts, and one book, Mari Sandoz's *Cheyenne Autumn* was made into a feature film in 1964. The movement of 1878 is as important to the Cheyenne as the Hebrew exodus from Egypt is to modern-day Jews, but in both cases, one must sift for the evidence.

SOUTH

In the summer of 1877, almost the entire Northern Cheyenne group went south, escorted by U.S. troops. They covered ground rapidly, but it was a long trip, about 1,100 miles (1,770 kilometers) to Fort Reno, in what is now Canadian County, Oklahoma. The move was accomplished without difficulty, but the Northern

Cheyenne were soon distressed and then appalled by what they found.

Only 50 years had passed since the Cheyenne had split into their northern and southern constituencies. The People—whether northern or southern—were much the same as before, but they had been forced, over two generations, to adapt to very different conditions. The Northern Cheyenne found the hot, dry Plains of what is now Oklahoma oppressive. They longed for the Northern Plains of what are now South Dakota and Montana. Unaccustomed to the climate, and susceptible to disease, the Northern Cheyenne lost more than 100 people—men, women, and children—in the year they spent around Fort Reno.

Making matters worse was the attitude of the U.S. government. The Bureau of Indian Affairs responded slowly to requests from Agent John D. Miles. A Quaker, Miles was interested in his charges and inclined to do his best for them, but the slow delivery of supplies—especially of promised annuities—made the Cheyenne extremely impatient. Working with Colonel Joseph Rendlebrock, commander of Fort Reno, Miles ordered a census taken of the Cheyenne, northern and southern alike. As he expressed it in a report to Washington D.C.:

> Every effort was made to assure them of our good intentions and to induce compliance with the order; but although a large majority of the band, including the women, would gladly have submitted and remained at the agency, the fighting element decided otherwise, and, in order to resist any effort at a compulsory count they began the work of entrenching in the sand-hills near their camps. (Miles's report was in the *New York Times* of October 13, 1878.)

Colonel Rendlebrock knew something of the valor of the Cheyenne. Rather than attack the entrenchments, he set up about 300 U.S. soldiers in areas around them, expecting to wait, or perhaps starve, the Cheyenne out. His expectation was defeated, according to Mari Sandoz in *Cheyenne Autumn,* when the entire group of Northern Cheyenne, about 350 in all, "quietly packed their ponies and struck north, leaving their lodges standing." This action, on the night of September 9, 1878, was the beginning of one of the most celebrated military actions of Native American history.

DULL KNIFE AND LITTLE WOLF

Both men were Northern Cheyenne chiefs, and both had been involved in the long struggle against the Anglo-American settlers. Neither entertained any thought of defeating the whites, who were far too numerous for the Cheyenne to ever prevail against. The profound longing for home (the Northern Plains) is what drove these two chiefs to lead their band of Northern Cheyenne out of the Indian agency and head north.

Historians have long been skeptical of Mari Sandoz's *Cheyenne Autumn.* First published in 1953, the book was hailed by those who like imaginative history, and denounced by others, who said its claims were overdrawn. There is no doubt that *Cheyenne Autumn* is a classic of literary history, however, and some words from Sandoz are in order:

> So the Indians vanished from the lodges under the veiling moon, going like the fox sneaking up a gully, not like the Cheyennes of the old days, bold as the gray wolf who stalks the ridges with his tail straight up in the air. The Cheyennes were not strong in warriors now. A year ago they brought two hundred fighting men along. But now barely a hundred remained, counting all over twelve, the age not for war but to take up weapons for defense. All the others were lost—many sick and dead from the hunger and fevers and the old, old disease of homesickness that no doctor, not even Bridge the medicine healer, had the power to cure.

So far, so good. The Cheyenne escaped the Fort Reno area and moved north, sometimes covering 35 miles (56 kilometers) a day. They moved by night as much as possible and sent out their scouts so they might know which ridges to avoid.

Colonel Rendlebrock pursued the Cheyenne with about 100 U.S. soldiers. Given that the refugees had women and children in great number, it seems incredible that it took Rendlebrock

Forced to abandon the Black Hills, the Cheyenne traveled more than a thousand miles south to their new reservation in Oklahoma, but decided after a year of death and hardship to escape back to their northern homeland.

three days to catch them. When he did, the Indians appeared to be cornered, boxed into a canyon. The Cheyenne had laid a trap, however, and Rendlebrock's advance party rode straight into it. The first bullets were fired by the Cheyenne, who, clearly, were not going to be taken back to the Fort Reno agency.

The Cheyenne won this first contest, in that they held Rendlebrock's men off, inflicting more casualties than they suffered. Rendlebrock had never been especially keen on his assignment in the first place, and after this first abortive attempt, he called off his pursuit. There were plenty of other regiments of U.S. soldiers between the Cheyenne and their northern destination, but Rendlebrock did not expect the sense of panic that swept the Southern Plains over the next few days.

Americans—whether eastern or western—were accustomed to thinking that the Indian wars were over: that the surrender of Crazy Horse and Chief Joseph—both in 1877—had brought the long conflicts to an end. Then, in the autumn of 1878, Americans were both interested and alarmed to hear that the Cheyenne were on the loose. The *New York Times* called it a "Great Indian Outbreak" on September 20:

> Dodge City, Kan. The most intense excitement prevails here over the attack of 300 Indians upon the cattle camp of Champan & Tuttle, 20 miles [32 kilometers] from here, and in which George Simmonds and a man whose name is not known were killed. Simmonds was in a wagon, and was literally riddled with arrows and bullets. The remainder of the men fled in the direction of Dodge City and were hotly pursued by the Indians.

The *New York Times* and its readers understood that these Indians were one band of Northern Cheyenne that had escaped from Indian Territory, but the first reports made it sound as if there was "rapine and murder in Kansas." The *New York Times* did not get it all wrong by any means, but its writers exaggerated the danger. On September 21, the *Times* labeled it the "Cheyenne Outbreak" and on October 26 it went so far as to call it the "Cheyenne

War." By then, most Anglo Americans knew of the action on the Great Plains, and some even held out sympathy for the Cheyenne who, after all, only wanted to return to their ancestral homeland.

INDIAN VIEWPOINT

The Cheyenne looked at the whole matter differently. To them, it was an exodus of necessity, prompted by the terrible climate in Indian Territory and the negligence of the Bureau of Indian Affairs. If they could reach their northern lands in peace, they would do so, but if they had to fight, they would. Even within their own number, there were divisions, however. Some of the younger men wanted to make real war upon the whites, while Chief Dull Knife and Little Wolf were intent on escape. Mari Sandoz, who obtained her information from descendants of the escaping Cheyenne, expresses it thus in *Cheyenne Autumn*:

> [Little Wolf] had more words, a whole harangue boiling up in his scarred breast where the medal of peace from the Great [White] Father hung, but he saw the forward straining of his divided followers, back in the shadows heard the cry of the women, their running for the children as the younger, wilder warriors of both sides moved against each other, knives out, guns up, tempers taut as dry bowstrings worn by the long flight. One finger's slipping and there would be blood in the canyon.

Little Wolf accepted the inevitable. The escaping Cheyenne divided into two groups, one under his leadership and the other following Dull Knife. Each group would continue on for sanctuary in the north.

RUN TO EARTH

Dull Knife and Little Wolf led their respective groups north, with the former going almost due north and the latter making a northwesterly hook on the way. By this time (mid-October), several thousand U.S. troops were on their trail. Average Americans laughed at the inability of the army to track down a few hundred

Following the Trail

In the spring of 1995, a time when Americans were dismayed by the explosion at a federal building in Oklahoma City, a professor of English from Vermont began to follow the trail of Little Wolf, Dull Knife, and the refugees of 1878. His name was Alan Boye, and the book he later wrote was *Holding Stone Hands: On the Trail of the Cheyenne Exodus.*

Boye began his route at Fort Reno. His brother dropped him off, and they made plans for the pickup about 1,100 miles (1,770 kilometers) in the north. Once he strode off, with a heavy backpack, Boye was on his own.

Almost from the start, Boye found encouragement and disbelief. He met Natives who were grandchildren of Chief Black Kettle, but he also encountered white Americans who thought he was crazy. Why did he wish to re-enact the movement of a group of Indians? Given his athletic ability (he had trained as a walker in the Green Mountains of Vermont), Boye would probably have covered the entire distance on his own, with difficulty, but he was fortunate to meet a handful of Northern Cheyenne. They had heard of his quest, and they came south from the Lame Deer reservation in Montana to join him. Boye describes his first meeting:

> He is a tall, slender man, whose walk is an easy, solid, and erect gait. He wears a felt black cowboy-style hat. He is an Indian.
>
> Although we have never met, there is no doubt about who the other might be.
>
> "Andrew," I say. His eyes briefly reach mine and we smile.
>
> "Alan," he says. On this remote and emptiest of back roads, Andrew Sootkis has found me.

This was the beginning of a wonderful three-way partnership, between Boye, Andrew Sootkis, and Sam Spotted Elk. Together they walked hundreds of miles, usually paralleled by several Cheyenne women in an automobile. They faced rattlesnakes in great number, sudden lightning storms, and more than a little danger from cars and trucks. They were determined to make a faithful tracing of the route, even if that meant going through inhospitable territory.

Sometimes they met wonderfully friendly people, who took them in and explained the significance of local historic sites. At other times they encountered suspicion, and sometimes outright hostility. One of Boye's frustrations was that so many journalists wanted to interview him, rather than his two Native fellow travelers. They reached their destination of Fort Robinson, and Boye continued on to see Bear Butte, the holy mountain of the Cheyenne. To his astonishment, Boye was adopted by one more fellow hiker, not a Cheyenne, not a Sioux, but a Japanese man who had been inspired by the film *Dances with Wolves*, which came out in 1990. This man spoke very little English, but his warm companionship and tremendous interest in the American West made for a strong bond between the two men. Boye reached the summit of Bear Butte in August.

As he neared the top, Boye had a sudden vision, or what appeared to be one. Sunlight was hitting the wings of hundreds of dragonflies, and for about 20 seconds Boye was in the midst of a vision. He wrote:

> The vision is even more powerful now that I have seen the dragonflies, for the light is alive with them. Despite it all, despite the world's ills and my own unpurified soul, there is grace in the universe. There is a grace, and for a moment on the Teaching Place—Noahvose—I am allowed to see this miracle for what it is: a canyon full of burning lights of a thousand tiny suns on the wings of star blue dragonflies.

When Dull Knife and his group of Cheyenne were told they were to return to the Cheyenne reservation in Oklahoma, they staged a stunning escape in the middle of night. Those that were caught were killed immediately. A group that was found in a dry creek bed was later massacred (*above*).

Cheyenne, and the entire matter was an embarrassment to the government.

Dull Knife's band was finally cornered, and forced to surrender, on October 25, 1878. Dull Knife and his fellow Cheyenne were taken to Fort Robinson in Nebraska, where their captors marveled at how lean and hungry these Indians were, and how many hardships they had endured in the struggle to reach their homeland. Unfortunately, the worst was yet to come.

Embarrassed that the Cheyenne had escaped from Indian Territory, the U.S. government decided to send them all back to present-day Oklahoma. This intention was voiced to Dull Knife, who replied in eloquent language, as cited in *Cheyenne Autumn*:

> We bowed to the will of the Great Father, and we went far into
> the south where he told us to go. There we found that a Cheyenne
> cannot live. We belong here. I knew this country before a one of
> your white men set his foot along our rivers, before he brought

his whiskey to our villages, or your bluecoats spurred along the trails, north and south. . . . Many times you promised us an agency, but you only took us far to the south country, saying, "Go and see. You can come back."

When the white commanders asked Dull Knife to reconsider, saying that they believed it was better for his people to yield on this point, he refused, saying, "I am here on my own ground, and I will never go back." Many of the U.S. soldiers were sympathetic, but the new garrison commander, Captain Henry Wessels, was not among them. He viewed the Cheyenne as incorrigible rebels, and around Christmastime of 1878, he had them locked in a wooden building from which only their leaders could exit, and only for a few hours at a time. To a people accustomed to the hardships of the Plains, and the desperate quest that led them north, this type of incarceration was the worst of all. In January 1879, they made a desperate attempt to escape.

The Cheyenne broke out at night, surprising the soldiers by coming out of the cellar with handmade weapons. Once past the guards, the Cheyenne scattered into the moonlit night. All the U.S. Army reports confirm that it was -40°F (-40°C), and the soldiers could not pursue the Cheyenne as far as they wished. Those who were caught were mostly killed, and some of their bodies were mutilated. The next morning saw the U.S. Cavalry come out in force, and the last survivors were trapped. They came to terrible ends, on a cold January day in 1879.

Ulysses S. Grant had left office two years earlier, and Rutherford B. Hayes was president of the United States. Both Grant and Hayes were honorable men, who would not have wished to inflict suffering on anyone they knew personally, but the great physical distance between the Great White Father in Washington, D.C., and his disobedient children on the Great Plains allowed for a large measure of cruelty.

As a military force, the Cheyenne were completely broken. As a symbol of what happened to Native Americans, they were a sad spectacle. As a cultural force, they remained intact.

Reservation Days

The 1880s and 1890s marked a major change for The People. Whether they were Northern Cheyenne, living in Montana, or Southern Cheyenne in Oklahoma, The People were confined to reservations. No longer were they the free agents of the open Plains.

THE NORTH

By 1880, a group of Northern Cheyenne who had had been able to avoid being taken south to Oklahoma three years earlier congregated in an area of southeastern Montana. They centered on the village of Lame Deer, named for one of the last Sioux chiefs to fight the whites.

Tradition has it that the Cheyenne were asked which section of the lands that remained was preferable to them and that they selected the Lame Deer area because there were still some buffalo in that region. In 1884, President Chester A. Arthur confirmed what had been promised; his presidential order set aside a large area (about 350,000 acres) around the Tongue River in southeastern Montana, with Lame Deer at the center. This, the president said, would be Cheyenne land forever. There were troubles right from the beginning, however.

The Cheyenne liked their new home, but they were not pleased to have the Crow Indian Reservation directly to the west. The two peoples had been foes "since time out of mind," and the Cheyenne and the Crow were wary of each other for the first two generations of reservation life. Over time, the two peoples became more accepting of each other, but plenty of disparaging words and jokes about the Crow were still made into the middle of the twentieth century. Worse than the proximity of the Crow was the influx of Anglo-American settlers from the east. John Stands in Timber expresses it thus:

> The Indians did not get to Tongue River very far ahead of the settlers. The first one, George Brewster, came in 1882, and a few more arrived each year. Several took up land before the reservation was [officially] established in 1884, and then were right in the middle of it. Not long after they came, the last buffalo were killed, and cattle began straying onto reservation land which was not yet fenced. Game was hard to find, and for a time the people were given no rations, so they began butchering those stray cattle.

As one would expect, this butchering caused tension between the whites and the Cheyenne, and in 1884, the first shooting took place. Because the white settler involved later wrote a book about her time in Montana, titled *A Bride Goes West*, there are several accounts, and most of them corroborate the main parts of the story.

The Alderson family had moved from West Virginia to Lame Deer, where it was one of the few Anglo-American groups within the reservation. The Aldersons were good people, and their

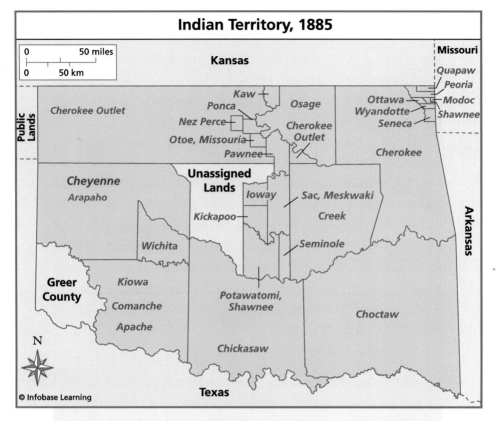

Indian Territory, 1885

0   50 miles

0   50 km

Public Lands

Missouri

Kansas

Quapaw

Peoria

Cherokee Outlet

Kaw

Ponca

Osage

Ottawa

Modoc

Wyandotte

Shawnee

Nez Perce

Seneca

Cherokee Outlet

Otoe, Missouria

Pawnee

Cherokee

Cheyenne

Arapaho

Unassigned Lands

Ioway

Sac, Meskwaki

Kickapoo

Creek

Wichita

Seminole

Arkansas

Greer County

Kiowa

Comanche

Potawatomi, Shawnee

Choctaw

Apache

N

Chickasaw

© Infobase Learning

Texas

The U.S. government attempted to combine the two groups of Cheyenne in Oklahoma, the reservation allotted to the Southern Cheyenne. The Northern Cheyenne found it impossible to adapt to the conditions of the Plains and returned to Montana.

relations with the Cheyenne were generally positive, but one of the cowboys who visited their farm took a shot at a Cheyenne lying on the ground. All accounts agree that the shooting was done as part of a bet ("I bet I can knock off that hat and not hit him"). This seemed harmless to the cowboys involved, but the old Cheyenne, Black Wolf, was creased on the forehead, and this incident brought out most of the Cheyenne within a 10-mile (16-kilometer) radius. The Aldersons got away unharmed, but their farm was burned to the ground and their possessions were taken. When U.S. soldiers arrived, they arrested four men. John Stands in Timber's father was one of the four who served prison terms for the burning of the farm. The incident seems small compared with the great battles of the 1860s and 1870s, but it long remained in the memories of the people of Montana, Indian and white alike.

Responding to claims of cattle filching and counterclaims of white encroachment on Indian land, the U.S. government worked hard to get at the truth. In the 1890s, a special investigator went to the Tongue River agency. He reported favorably on the Cheyenne, saying that they suffered—and quietly endured—more bad treatment than they gave. In 1900, President William McKinley put the ink on a final declaration, which increased the size of the Tongue River reservation to about 440,000 acres and made plain that this would remain Indian land. It was around that time that the Cheyenne began to raise cattle.

Raising beef cattle had never been a favorite occupation of the Cheyenne, who remembered Sweet Medicine's words about a strange animal with pointed hooves. The economic demands of the late-nineteenth century, however, persuaded many of them to begin cattle ranching, and from the very beginning they showed a talent for it. The U.S. government was skeptical at first, but early in the twentieth century, Washington, D.C., sent a small number of surplus cattle to the Tongue River reservation, and The People began to prosper. Some of the meat from their ranches went all the way to the stockyards in Chicago.

ALLOTMENT

Meanwhile, a well-intentioned government policy was wreaking havoc with many Native groups, including the Cheyenne. In 1887, Congress passed the Indian General Allotment Act (often called the Dawes Act in honor of its sponsoring congressman). Under its provisions, many Indians—throughout the United States— were required to surrender their reservation lands in return for allotments of 160 acres (for a head of household), 80 acres (for a

---

A Family and its Neighbors

Nannie T. Alderson's *A Bride Goes West* attracted much attention when it was published in 1942. Americans were then in the middle of World War II, and the relatively mundane difficulties of a farmer's wife in eastern Montana seemed rather remote, perhaps even quaint.

Recounting events from a half-century earlier, Alderson depicted the rugged, harsh beauty of life on the Plains. She and her husband moved from West Virginia to the Montana Territory in 1882, thereby coinciding with the selection of the Lame Deer area as the Northern Cheyenne reservation. Alderson did not explain how she and her husband (they had three children) ended up in Lame Deer, with mostly Indian neighbors, but her writing does display the marked differences between Native American and Anglo-American cultures. She wrote:

> It was all very kindly up to a point, but beyond the kindness there was a blank wall. In view of the cruelties that had been exchanged between white man and Indian, it was no wonder if real warmth was lacking between them, or if the Indian attitude toward us was one of complete cynicism. I can understand this now, but at the time I was

single adult), and 40 acres (for an underage person). The Allotment Act did not harm the Northern Cheyenne, because the Tongue River reservation was so well established, but the same cannot be said for their southern cousins.

THE SOUTH

Life for the Southern Cheyenne was, if anything, more difficult than for their northern kinsmen. The two peoples still considered themselves one tribal entity, but the physical distance had

terrible disappointed. I came from the South, and despite
the burning of our house I looked, unconsciously perhaps,
for the same affectionate relationship with the Indians that
had existed in my old home between the colored people
and the whites.

No twenty-first century publisher would bring out a book
with words like these, but it is valuable to examine them to
see the attitudes of Anglo Americans in the 1880s and 1890s.
Alderson displayed a paternalistic attitude, hoping that the
Native Americans would be compliant and easygoing, like
the African Americans she knew in West Virginia. Very likely,
she deceived herself about black-white relations in the
American South, and, very likely, she could not understand
the intricacies of Indian-Anglo relations in the West.

She did note that the Cheyenne were expert in the management of children. Unlike white settlers, who sometimes
administered physical punishment, the Indians would "snatch
them out of mischief, give them a little shake and grunt at
them, and there it ends. After that the child is simply removed
from temptation, and I have never seen one of them spank a
small child." White fur traders had made similar observations
as early as the 1850s. The Cheyenne form of child-rearing
was singularly gentle, they said, and the Indians believed that
to shout at or punish a child was harmful to his or her spirit.

increased, and there were now railroads and cattle herds, as well as
roads and pioneers in between.

To the Cheyenne, the difference—or separation—was sym-
bolized by the Four Sacred Arrows staying in the south and the
Sacred Buffalo Hat remaining in the north. The two Cheyenne
groups were effectively cut off from one another by geography, but
their belief in the sacred items remained strong.

In his book *The Cheyenne and Arapaho Ordeal*, Donald J. Berthrong describes both the well-intentioned efforts of some white

The Southern Cheyenne in Oklahoma were constantly overrun by settlers who were trying to carve out a piece of land for themselves. Land runs (*above*), races that awarded plots of land on a first-come, first-served basis, were a popular event in Oklahoma.

Indian agents and the desire of many white Oklahomans to remove the Southern Cheyenne entirely. Some nefarious negotiations took place in 1890 and 1891, with some Southern Cheyenne resisting and others giving in to the allotment of their land (160 acres per family) and then the sale of the remaining lands for $1.5 million. At the time, $1.5 million was quite enticing, but, as the Cheyenne soon discovered, it was a bad bargain.

The Southern Cheyenne were in the northwest corner of the Indian Territory when it was opened to white settlement in the great Land Run of 1892. The story of how the white settlers charged over the starting line and lunged many miles that day has been told many times; but the subsequent loss of land to the Cherokee, Cheyenne, and other tribes in the territory is usually ignored. The Southern Cheyenne did not lose much land in the initial push, but as white towns and farms sprang up around them, the Cheyenne experienced difficulties similar to those of their northern cousins. By about 1900, the Southern Cheyenne were locked into their section of what had become the State of Oklahoma.

The Southern Cheyenne generally had it worse than their northern counterparts. So many Anglo Americans were moving into Oklahoma (which became a state in 1907) that the Southern Cheyenne had no way to build a strong land base. What eventually became the Cheyenne-Arapaho Reservation was smaller than the Northern Cheyenne Indian Reservation in Montana; worse, it was split, unevenly, so that the Cheyenne lived in no fewer than eight counties of Oklahoma.

By 1914, the two Cheyenne groups had made an agreement about the sacred objects of the tribe. The Sacred Buffalo Hat would remain in the north, and the Four Sacred Arrows would remain in the south.

THE PEOPLE IN 1914

The People were in a mixed state in 1914. The cattle-ranching experiment in Montana had been a major success, to such a degree that many white cattle ranchers were eager to have the Northern Cheyenne removed. The People were taking too much business, and profit, away from their white rivals.

The Tongue River reservation had been established in 1884 and confirmed in 1900. There was no question it would remain, but there was a question as to how close the white settlers would come. The reservations of the Southern Cheyenne were in worse shape. They did not have the iron-clad certainty of a presidential order creating their existence, and it was possible that white Oklahoma farmers would manage to have them removed, although one could certainly ask: To where? There was not much "open" land remaining, even in the West.

In 1914, the Northern Cheyenne sent a special delegation to Washington, D.C., to meet President Woodrow Wilson. The first Democrat elected since 1892, Wilson had the reputation of being a reformer and a "do-gooder," but, as the African-American community had learned, Wilson's largesse did not extend to minorities. The Cheyenne delegation made no headway concerning cattle and land rights; the Bureau of Indian Affairs was already considering how it might remove the successful Indian entrepreneurs it had created. Then, just as things seemed to get better, the Great War began.

World Wars and the Great Depression

The beginning of World War I—known as the Great War—found the Northern Cheyenne in the strongest condition of the past 50 years. The same cannot be said for the Southern Cheyenne, who were mired in economic difficulties. Both groups experienced World War I as a time of important change.

MILITARY SERVICE DURING WORLD WAR I

Europe exploded into war in the summer of 1914, but the United States did not enter until April 1917. It was lost on no one—especially the Northern Cheyenne—that one of the few votes against the war (in the U.S. House of Representatives) was cast by Jeannette Rankin, a Montana rancher who had just become the first woman to serve in either house of Congress. This pacifistic gesture did not influence the Cheyenne very much, however, because they had a warrior tradition in their tribe. Some of the

Cheyenne of 1917 had fathers and grandfathers who had served as scouts for the U.S. Army after the general surrender of 1877. The Cheyenne of 1917 continued their familial and tribal tradition of military service.

Few hard statistics exist for the Cheyenne in this period, but U.S. records indicate that 11,803 Native American men registered for the Selective Service and that 6,509 were inducted. This means that about 55 percent of all Indians who registered served in some capacity, and records show that another 5,500 Native Americans registered after September 1918. How many of these were Cheyenne is not known, but in the immediate aftermath of the war, a new Dog Soldier Society was formed in western Oklahoma. Those Cheyenne who went overseas were fortunate to see a different part of the world, and those who returned had many stories to tell their families. Thanks to the efforts Native Americans made during World War I, Congress took action in 1924, making all Natives U.S. citizens.

World War I ended in November 1918. The war that had been fought to "make the world safe for democracy" (in President Woodrow Wilson's words) was over. The Cheyenne—northern and southern—were about to face new enemies, and this time they were shared with their white neighbors.

Influenza appeared in the United States in October and November 1918. The "Spanish Flu," as it was called, claimed about 650,000 American lives over the next six months, far more than had been lost to combat in World War I. The Cheyenne seemed remote, far from the cause of illness, but they, too, suffered; it is believed that several hundred of The People died in 1918 and 1919. The combined population of Northern and Southern Cheyenne fell to its lowest level since records were kept. One more affliction was in store.

The winters of 1919 and 1920 were exceptionally cold. Many cattle died on the Northern Cheyenne Indian Reservation and many horses, as well. Deeply attached to their animals, the Cheyenne mourned the losses. The Northern Cheyenne cattle herd did not return to its pre–World War I level, and The People suffered more economic hardship. It was around this time that the Cheyenne experienced a newcomer to the Great Plains, one that would influence their lives almost as much as the horse had in the nineteenth century.

HORSES, CATTLE, AND CARS

No one knows which Cheyenne had the first automobile, but we suspect that he or she was the object of much flattery and attention for the next several years. Automobiles had appeared on the East Coast as early as 1905, but it was during the early 1920s that cars came to the Great Plains, and the Cheyenne welcomed this newcomer with fascination.

Until about 1925, Cheyenne life was dependent on the horse-drawn wagon. Like their ancestors, who had fearlessly covered great distances by horseback, the early-twentieth-century Cheyenne made long trips by wagon, including visits between the northern and southern tribal groups. When the automobile appeared, however, the Cheyenne were entranced. Charles Penoi describes it in *No More Buffaloes*:

> The automobile has replaced the horse as the number one love of the Cheyenne and Arapaho. If they have any money it will go for a car and gasoline; no other object gives the same status. Automobiles are owned by most families. In some cases they are jokingly called "Indian cars." Some of the windows have been knocked out and replaced with cardboard; the tires are slick; the bodies are dented and scratched and are seldom washed. The only concern is—will it run?

Penoi notes that, while Cheyenne families will take each other in, and feed one another at no charge, automobiles are the one exception to the rule. Those who ride in others' cars are expected to pay for gasoline, and passengers are expected to buy their driver's food.

Of course the Cheyenne were not that different from twentieth-century white Americans, who also developed a tremendous love for the automobile. But there was something special in the Cheyenne adoration of the car, because it was the replacement—in some way—of the horse, which had been so important to them a century earlier.

THE TWENTIES

Americans remember the "Roaring Twenties" fondly, as a time of new music, new appliances, and an overall joyful approach to life. Many Cheyenne feel similarly. To them, the 1920s were the good old times, when The People had enough in the way of material goods and did not feel separate from the culture of their ancestors.

Though the cattle and horse herds were much reduced by the terrible winters of 1919 and 1920, the Northern and Southern Cheyenne derived a significant income from a combination of cattle-raising and farming during the 1920s. The automobile was changing their lives, but almost no one saw any negative side to the change. Only later, in retrospect, did some older Cheyenne claim that the automobile had a negative consequence for social life: As Betty Sue Flowers expressed it, as recorded in *The Road to Lame Deer*, "When the car came, people stopped visiting." On the whole, the Cheyenne experienced decent economic times in the 1920s, and they still maintained a strong connection to the free and wild life of their grandparents. The fiftieth anniversary of Custer's Last Stand, for example, provided the opportunity for a number of Cheyenne to give talks on the battlefield and to make markers to show where their comrades had fallen. This was also a time when the first white photographers appeared on the Cheyenne reservations, and, thanks to some of them, the first large number of photographs was made and preserved.

Thomas B. Marquis was a white physician who arrived at Lame Deer in eastern Montana in 1925, intending to serve as a doctor to the Northern Cheyenne community. He found that the large distances to cover were too much, and he stopped practicing medicine after less than a year. Fascinated by the Cheyenne, Marquis began to take photographs of men, women, and children. Some were developed at the time and shown to The People, but others rusted away in trunks for many years before being rescued. Not until 2006 were the photographs compiled into *A Northern Cheyenne Album*, one of the most remarkable photographic portraits of a tribal people. The written commentary was provided by Cheyenne leader John Woodenlegs, who was given Marquis's negatives after the physician's death.

To the best of our knowledge, the Cheyenne had been rather "dry" until the 1920s. There had been few incidents involving drunkenness. But the 1920s—the decade in which the United States experimented with Prohibition—provided many temptations. Not only was the automobile available to carry Cheyenne greater distances, but there were more illegal places to obtain alcohol. Whatever the reason, the Cheyenne began to drink, and scenes from the Tongue River area were less appealing than before. At precisely the time that Thomas B. Marquis preserved the vision of an unspoiled way of life, that pastoral scenery began to be enmeshed with the scars of alcoholism.

THE GREAT DEPRESSION

The Great Depression of 1929–1941 hit the Cheyenne hard. They had just come up in the world, experiencing a mild prosperity for the first time, when the circumstances of the 1930s threw them backward. Automobiles remained a feature of Cheyenne life, but they tended to be very run-down and sometimes decrepit in appearance. The tribal herds of horses and cows remained about the same size, but the beef that was shipped to Chicago earned a much lower price than before. Public health also took a turn for the worse.

One reason the Northern Cheyenne had fled the South in 1878 was the high rate of disease, malaria especially. The Northern

John Woodenlegs (1909–1981)

Born on the Northern Cheyenne Indian Reservation in 1909, John Woodenlegs was the grandson of Wooden Leg, whose description of the Battle of the Little Bighorn is one of the best we have from the Native point of view. John Woodenlegs was born during what many Northern Cheyenne call the "good old days," and his memories often reflect that attitude. In old age, when he was asked to comment on a large number of Thomas B. Marquis photographs, Woodenlegs was able to identify people, buildings, and places, but the most telling commentary he made was usually on people's character: "They were all good people," he was fond of saying.

Woodenlegs became leader of the Native American Church on the reservation in the 1940s, and for the rest of his life he was referred to as a "road man," meaning the person who led peyote ceremonies, many of which went on from Saturday evening until early Sunday morning. He was also elected tribal president of the Northern Cheyenne, holding that position for almost 20 years. As president, Woodenlegs saw the transition from an isolated reservation to one informed by the return of Korean War and Vietnam War veterans. His biggest error,

Cheyenne were a hearty, healthy people until the Great Depression, when several circumstances combined against them. The reduction in cattle-raising meant there was less meat. Second, many Cheyenne had become accustomed to the rather modest handouts from the U.S. government. Third, the Cheyenne diet changed. Charles Penoi describes a typical diet in a Southern Cheyenne home in Oklahoma:

> Like most Plains Indians, Cheyennes and Arapahos are meat eaters. They learned that meat was a source of strength. . . . In

if one wants to label it so, was the acceptance of leases with the major coal companies. Neither Woodenlegs nor his fellow council members understood all the legalese in the documents that were signed in 1973, and he was later active in having them revoked.

Woodenlegs had many achievements of which to be proud, but he was, perhaps, keenest on his role in Cheyenne education. He founded Dull Knife Memorial College in 1975, even though the entire tribal education budget had been only $600 a year when he first became president. The library of the new college, which was renamed Chief Dull Knife College in 2001, was named for him. Woodenlegs himself graduated from the University of Montana in 1978, one of the first members of the Northern Cheyenne to do so.

Woodenlegs died in Billings, Montana, in December 1981. Twenty-eight years later, his memory was resurrected in an odd fashion. Former vice-presidential candidate Sarah Palin, in her memoir *Going Rogue*, quoted John Woodenlegs to this degree: "Our land is everything to us. . . . I will tell you one of the things we remember on our land. We remember our grandfathers paid for it—with their *lives*."

Ironically, Palin attributed the quotation to John Wooden, the legendary basketball coach of UCLA.

addition to meat, they eat store bread and coffee with very few vegetables. Like their counterpart in the non-Indian world, most children would rather have a hamburger, French fries, and a Coca-Cola. Babies are about the only members of the family that drink milk.

This is, of course, a generalization, and some Cheyenne continued to eat well-balanced meals. On the whole, however, Plains Indians—with their long history of eating meat—were particularly susceptible to a diet heavy in protein and carbohydrates, without enough green vegetables. The result has been a major increase in the onset of juvenile and adult diabetes.

DUST BOWL

If alcoholism and an unbalanced diet affected most of the Cheyenne (Northern and Southern), the Southern Cheyenne faced one very special obstacle in the 1930s: the Dust Bowl.

Beginning in 1934, the southern part of the Great Plains experienced the worst drought seen in centuries. Dust—kicked up by wind—spread all over the states of Oklahoma and Texas, bringing a cruel new enemy to the Southern Cheyenne. They did

The Great Depression and the Dust Bowl added to the hardships of the Southern Cheyenne in Oklahoma. Drought, irresponsible farming, and overgrazing caused terrible dust storms, leaving many Indians and non-Indians with lung and respiratory problems.

not suffer any more than their white counterparts, but there were few doctors and almost no hospitals in their area. Hundreds of Southern Cheyenne may have suffered permanent lung damage as a result of ingesting dirt. To a people who pride themselves on strength and endurance, the resulting weakness may have been psychologically, as well as physically, devastating.

Alcoholism, diet, the Great Depression, and the Dust Bowl all took a terrible toll on the Cheyenne during the 1930s. For the first time, however, they had a friend in Washington, D.C.

INDIAN REORGANIZATION ACT

In 1933, President Franklin D. Roosevelt nominated John Collier as commissioner of Indian affairs. A social worker by training and an idealist by nature, Collier was interested in Native Americans *as they were* rather than as latecomers to white society. Seeing much good in the Indian societies of the nineteenth century, Collier wanted to assist tribes in preserving their heritage. With his legislative work, and with President Roosevelt behind him, Collier drafted the Indian Reorganization Act, which passed Congress in 1934.

Under the IRA, the allotment system was abandoned. Allotment had never really harmed the Northern Cheyenne, but the Southern Cheyenne had lost as much as three million acres of land during the long allotment period (1887–1934). Further losses were prevented, but there was no way to go back and regain what had been taken.

On the positive side, the IRA created a large-scale lending program. The Northern Cheyenne were particularly successful in obtaining funds: One scholar estimates that they received more in loans than any other tribe nationwide. The Cheyenne increased the size of their horse and cattle herds, and undertook irrigation improvements. The Southern Cheyenne and the Arapaho were not as successful, perhaps because they had less land on which to draw. In both cases, however, the Indian Reorganization Act was generally seen as an improvement. One negative, from the traditional point of view, was that the IRA called for tribal organizations, elections, and a more "modern" approach to tribal government. The elections were held, and the Northern Cheyenne and the Southern Cheyenne and Arapaho had tribal presidents and councils for the first time. This meant that their traditional leaders—the tribal chiefs—had much less influence than before. Loretta Fowler describes a particular vignette, from 1933, in *Tribal Sovereignty and the Historical Imagination*:

> Five elderly Arapaho chiefs traveled to the agency office at Concho [Oklahoma] to talk to Superintendent L.S. Bonnin. Little Raven Jr. had made the seventy-mile trip from Canton to urge the superintendent to persuade the commissioner of Indian affairs to support an extension of the trust status of the Cheyenne and Arapaho lands beyond 1937. Bonnin refused to discuss the matter, insisting that only the elected representatives of a tribal council he organized in 1928 would be heard. Shocked, Little Raven Jr. exclaimed, "Am I a Chief?"

The answer, from the Indian Affairs bureaucrat, was that Little Raven Jr. was only an honorary chief. According to the new rules, established by the tribal government, the tribal council now superseded all previous forms of leadership.

THE CHEYENNE IN 1940

On the eve of the Second World War, the Cheyenne lived lives somewhat different from their parents, and dramatically different from their grandparents. There was plenty of veneration for the older generations, especially the handful of Cheyenne who could still recall fighting the U.S. Cavalry in the 1870s. For the most part, however, the Cheyenne—whether northern or southern—saw the necessity of entering the twentieth century, and doing so in a way that would enhance their status. Plenty of challenges remained:

Would there be sufficient economic opportunity?

Would the Cheyenne be able to enter white society
without losing their own?
Could the Cheyenne ever reunite their northern and
southern parts?

The answers to these questions, and others, hinged on the second great war, which was about to erupt.

World War II began with Hitler's invasion of Poland in September 1939, but the United States did not enter until December 1941, when the Japanese attacked the naval base at Pearl Harbor, Hawaii. To the best of historical knowledge, the Cheyenne were already entering the U.S. armed services prior to the attack.

WAR SERVICE

Hundreds of Cheyenne—men and women—served in World War II. Not all of their names are known to us, but happily we can list some of those who served. Lieutenant Richard Balenti won the Distinguished Flying Cross. Men like Sam Dives Backwards and Wesley Osage gave their lives (in the Philippines), while others such as Roy Nightwalker and Roy Bull Coming performed heroically on the European front. To the best of historical knowledge, many Cheyenne soldiers acted parts of their ancestral heritage in war; Roy Bull Coming, for example, delighted in counting coup on surprised German soldiers in the days following the D-Day invasion of Normandy. Perhaps the best-known World War II hero was John Greaney Jr., a Southern Cheyenne who fought with distinction on Iwo Jima. As cited in John Moore's *The Cheyenne*, the U.S. government magazine *Indians at Work* described a special homecoming for Greaney, held near El Reno, Oklahoma, in May 1945:

> 600 Indians, representing twelve tribes in the western part of
> the state, held an all-day victory celebration. . . . In an ancient
> sacred ceremony conducted by Ralph White Tail, a holy man of
> the Cheyenne, Greaney's Indian name was changed from Red

Many Native Americans, including hundreds of Cheyenne, served in World War I and World War II. (*Above*) A group of Native American Marines poses for a photo on the Pacific Island of Bougainville.

Tooth to Little Chief in recognition of the warrior's valorous deeds. This was followed by a "give away," and many valuable presents, including three horses, were distributed through the honored one. . . . Thereafter special victory dances, also led by the hero, were performed for the War Mothers, upon whose brilliantly colored shawls the names, ranks, and organizations of their warrior children were written that the world might see.

The Cheyenne soldiers and nurses (a number of Cheyenne women served in the Women's Army Corps) are not as well known as the Navajo Code Talkers, but they are part of a proud Cheyenne tradition: service in the U.S. military. Some of their grandparents had been scouts with the U.S. Army after the general surrender of 1877. There was another aspect to the Cheyenne war effort, though. In the summer of 1945, a small group of Northern Cheyenne went to Noahvose (the Holy Mountain) to pray for an end to the war. A local white farmer was so impressed that he offered them free passage across his land, and a tradition began of good relations between the Cheyenne and their white neighbors in the vicinity of the Holy Mountain.

The Cheyenne Today

It is often noted that the overall status of African Americans improved after World War II. The same cannot be said for most Native Americans who fought; upon returning home, they found conditions unchanged.

At the beginning of the presidency of Dwight D. Eisenhower, Termination became the official policy of the U.S. government. To terminate meant to end Native American sovereignty on reservations. Numerous tribes came in for prolonged legal assaults by the U.S. government, which hoped to break up the reservations and have the tribal peoples assimilate into the mainstream. Neither the Northern nor Southern Cheyenne suffered much during Termination, perhaps because their lands were not seen as that valuable. Oddly enough, it was during the Termination Era that the Cheyenne found one of their greatest admirers and strongest friends from white-American society: Father Peter J. Powell.

An ordained Episcopal priest, Father Powell was in his thirties when his fascination with the Cheyenne began. He spent a good deal of time on or near the Northern Cheyenne Reservation, and, in 1959, he was one of the first white people ever to be present when the Sacred Buffalo Hat was opened. Father Powell wrote about the experience in *Sweet Medicine*:

> Little Coyote untied the offering cloths and Last Bull lifted them from the bundle, assisted by Woodenlegs. The Buffalo priest said to Woodenlegs: "Watch the things as I get them out, so when I put them back you can remind me in what order they go back in."

The medicine bundle was opened on the fifth motion—symbolizing the importance of the four directions and Mother Earth. Father Powell's description continues:

> A bundle wrapped with a blue cloth followed. The five missing scalps were inside it! They were graduated in size and laced to wooden hoops. Tradition states that they were captured from the traditional enemies of the Suhtaio: the Crows, Shoshones, Utes, Pawnees, and Apaches.

The scalps indicate the long military heritage of the Cheyenne, but the Sacred Buffalo Hat is primarily a symbol of *female* power, granting life-giving energy to the women of the tribe. That is why the mutilation of the hat in 1874 had been so serious. The ritual continues:

> *Is'siwun* rested there, facing east. The "old animal hide"— probably mink or otter—was removed next. This was followed by a package of long twist tobacco—the old-time trade tobacco. Finally, Last Bull removed a bundle of fluffy white material, resembling animal fur, wrapped in a yellow checkered cloth. This material was said to be the wool of the yellow buffalo calf, the youngest member of the Buffalo Family. Now the opening of the Sacred Hat bundle was completed.

The opening of the Sacred Buffalo Hat did not make the "news" of the summer of 1959. Americans were occupied with other things, including the looming space race with the Soviet Union. Only with the passage of time—and the publication of Father Peter J. Powell's books—did it become clear how unusual the Cheyenne ceremonies were, and how fortunate The People were to have kept their traditions intact.

This did not mean there were no dangers to the heritage, however.

RED POWER

In the 1960s, a number of Native groups emerged, many with the same overall theme. They wanted their fellow Native Americans to take pride in their Indian status, and to encourage the preservation of Native culture throughout the United States. There was a more ominous-sounding aspect to the movement, though, and white Americans often associated the words *Red Power* with violent images of other minority groups (such as the Black Panthers) that spoke of overthrow of the U.S. government.

There were very few incidents on the Northern Cheyenne Reservation or in the Cheyenne-Arapaho towns of western Oklahoma. Perhaps this is because the traditional Cheyenne leadership had stayed intact through the twentieth century. Then again, it may be because the Cheyenne were distant from urban centers, where Red Power was more active. In either case, the Cheyenne did not "rise up" during the 1960s, and it took a major event in the 1970s to bring great concern to The People. The danger took the form of major coal companies that wanted to exploit Cheyenne land for the rich minerals beneath the soil.

BIG COAL

In the 1960s, several large coal companies discovered that the Northern Cheyenne and Crow reservations sat atop some of the richest deposits of bituminous (soft) coal to be found in North

America. With that discovery came a paradox. Might the Northern Cheyenne sell all, or part, of their reservation? If so, what
would happen to them as a people?

Controversy remains as to how the process started. Did the
Bureau of Land Management sell the Northern Cheyenne short,
or were the coal leases signed in the early 1970s the result of legiti-
mate negotiation between the Northern Cheyenne and the coal
companies? In either case, the Northern Cheyenne awoke to the
danger, and for several years there were standoffs between Native
activists and the bulldozers and plows of the companies collec-
tively known as "Big Coal." Thanks to the efforts of people like
Gail Small, who would go on to be the director of the law firm
Native Action, the Cheyenne won a major court victory in 1978.
The leases signed earlier in the decade were terminated, and the
Cheyenne again owned the totality of their 440,000-acre reservation. The onslaught continued, however.

Possessing large amounts of land in Rosebud County, just
north of the Northern Cheyenne Indian Reservation, the coal
companies drew up plans for 75,000 wells to be dug right on the
border. By about the year 2000, the companies were less interested
in the coal that existed and were keener on the natural gas that
could be brought up through pre-existing drill sites. By that year,
the coal companies were pumping as much as six billion gallons
of water—coming from the coal shafts—into local rivers. No one
knew for certain what the environmental impact would be.

As Gail Small expressed it, in the documentary film *Native
Action*, every member of the Northern Cheyenne tribe could
become a millionaire overnight, if the tribe decided to sell most of
its land to the coal companies. Given that the coal and natural gas
below were estimated to be worth $200 billion, it would be rela-
tively easy for Big Coal to offer a million or more to each Northern
Cheyenne: man, woman, and child. Since most people on the reservation had an annual income of about $10,000, well below the
poverty line, the potential buyout was an enormous temptation.

Gail Small (1956–)

Since the time of Sweet Medicine, perhaps even before, men have always led the Cheyenne. Even if women exerted a powerful influence behind the scenes, the council of 44 chiefs, and practically every other visible authority group, was composed of men. Something has changed, however, and women have stepped up to take a new, more visible role.

Born on the Northern Cheyenne Indian Reservation in 1956, Gail Small is a niece of John Woodenlegs, the legendary author, educator, and spiritual leader of the Northern Cheyenne during the 1950s and 1960s. Blessed with a sharp mind, Small was one of the first Cheyenne women to get an advanced education; by a wonderful coincidence, she and her uncle, John Woodenlegs, both received their bachelor's degrees from the University of Montana in 1978. The 1970s were a potent time for Small and the Northern Cheyenne as a whole, because that was the decade when the Big Coal companies made serious inroads on the reservation, leasing large sections of land.

Small and her uncle (who died in 1981) fought back. They were among the fiercest opponents of Big Coal, arguing that if what the Northern Cheyenne possessed was so wonderful, then it would only appreciate in value over time. The Cheyenne, they said, should be in no hurry to lease or sell any of their land. Encouraged by the legal victory over the coal

At the time of this writing, the Northern Cheyenne had not opened any part of their reservation to Big Coal. The People continued to live in a way that honored the land and the sacrifices their ancestors had made to obtain it. No one could say what the future will bring, however.

companies in 1978, Small went on to the University of Oregon School of Law, and she returned to the reservation as the tribe's first Juris Doctor (Doctor of Law).

The mother of four, and the founder of Native Action, a non-profit legal group, Small could have rested on her laurels. The appearance of a new possible profit to the coal companies necessitated her presence, however. The same companies that had hungered for the reservation's coal in the 1970s were keener on its coal-bed methane by around 2000. Tempting offers were made, to the extent which Small claimed that every man, woman, and child of the Northern Cheyenne could become a millionaire overnight, if the tribe was willing to sign away the rights to its land.

As of this writing, the Northern Cheyenne had not yet sold or leased land to the coal companies, but every member of the tribe can see the massive wells and refining pits that Big Coal has placed near the reservation. As Small said in an interview with *Sierra* magazine, The People have a momentous choice ahead of them.

"Cheyenne know their life on this earth is fleeting, and they look at the perpetuation of the tribe as the main goal. We want our culture, land, and language to live on. Getting methane wealth, seizing and conquering, living only for yourself—what do these things matter compared to the perpetuity of your people?" Small said. At times she was even pithier, simply saying, "Is our homeland going to be one big dump or a place we can live?"

THE HOLY MOUNTAIN

In 1961, the State of South Dakota established Bear Butte State Park, encompassing the area around Noahvose (the Holy Mountain). Making matters worse was the enlargement of the nearby annual motorcycle rally at Sturgis, South Dakota.

Bear Butte, the sacred mountain to both the Cheyenne and the Lakota Sioux, has been under constant threat of development. Business people have long since coveted the land and the valuable natural resources of the area.

The Sturgis Rally began in 1940 or 1941, at a time when the Indian Head Motorcycle (manufactured in Springfield, Massachusetts) was the favorite of many aficionados. Times change, however, and by the early twenty-first century, Harleys and Hondas dominated the rally, which is only a few miles from the holy mountain. Numerous issues evolved out of this close proximity between the sacred mountain and the rally, which one can say was sacred to many of its participants. One of the biggest problems had to do with noise. Garret Keizer describes it in *The Unwanted Sound of Everything We Want*:

> The resentment [between the Cheyenne and the motorcyclists] came to a head in 2006 when an Arizona-based entrepreneur and bike enthusiast Jay Allen purchased a 600-acre track on the

north side of the butte and declared his intention to build an outdoor rock amphitheatre and the "world's largest bike bar," which he intended to call Sacred Ground and mark with an 80-foot statue of an Indian.

Allen eventually changed the name to The County Line. He got his biker bar built, with the help of a Native American construction crew, some people said. The development did not stop the controversy. There have been repeated attempts to boycott The County Line.

LOSS OF LANGUAGE

Yet another area of concern is the slow, creeping loss of the Cheyenne tongue. As recently as 1925, at least half of all Cheyenne—northern, southern, or elsewhere—still spoke the language of their ancestors, but by 2010, it may have shrunk to as little as 10 percent. There has been no real replacement for men like John Woodenlegs and John Stands in Timber, either. There was even a concern that the most sacred objects might not have keepers for the future.

CONTINUATION OF TRADITION

There are bright spots, just the same. In the last decade of the twentieth century and the first decade of the twenty-first, Native culture rebounded in numerous ways, and the Cheyenne were no exception. In no special order, the cultural renaissance can be shown in the following ways:

- Powwows
- Continuation of Sacred Arrows and Buffalo Hat ceremonies
- Creation of new tribal customs

Powwows had long been part of Native lifestyles, but they became much more popular—attended by Natives and whites alike—early in the twenty-first century. The Sacred Arrows and Sacred Buffalo Hat ceremonies are very old indeed, but they were attended with greater reverence than in earlier times. Finally, the Cheyenne of 2010 were on the cusp of creating some new ceremonies, those that celebrated their past and pointed a way for what it was to be Cheyenne in the twenty-first century.

SUCCESS STORIES

The story of The People in the late twentieth and early twenty-first centuries is a mixed one, with hardship and loss alternating with enthusiasm and pride. There have been a number of individual success stories, as opposed to tribal ones, and those who have "made it" in the larger white society have provided inspiration to their fellow Cheyenne.

Born in California in 1933, Ben Nighthorse Campbell is the son of a Northern Cheyenne father and a Portuguese mother. He spent time on several reservations in his youth—including the adjacent Crow Reservation in southern Montana—but his upward mobility commenced through service in the U.S. Air Force. Campbell became a businessman before entering politics, and in 1992 he was elected to the U.S. Senate, representing Colorado. Originally a Democrat, Campbell switched to the Republican Party in 1995. When his political career in Washington ended, in 2005, he returned home to serve as a member of the Northern Cheyenne Council of 44.

Suzan Shown Harjo (born in 1945) is another striking success story. Born in Oklahoma to a Cheyenne father and a Creek/ Muskogee mother, she came of age during the Red Power movement of the 1960s and was appointed by President Jimmy Carter as a congressional liaison for Indian affairs. As president of the Morning Star Institute, Harjo has played a leading role in making Native American customs better known to the general public and to securing the repatriation of many bodies of Native Americans.

Success stories like these indicate that the Cheyenne have come a long way since the early twentieth century, when many

whites believed that they—and other Native American peoples—
would simply disappear.

SACRED ARROWS

Ever since Sweet Medicine returned from the Holy Mountain, the
Four Sacred Arrows have been the most prized possession of the
Cheyenne. True, the Pawnee captured three of the four arrows in
1830, and the tribal leaders had to "remake" three more to replace
them. Even so, the Four Sacred Arrows remain the strongest connection between Maheo and The People.

A number of men have served as Keeper of the Sacred Arrows
over the centuries. At the time of this writing, the arrows were
kept by William Wayne Red Hat Jr., living in Longdale, Oklahoma. Red Hat was the third member of his family to have been
the Keeper. In 2003, anthropologist Sibylle M. Schlesier inter-
viewed him at length:

> My grandmother's grandfather was also Arrow Keeper. It is
> interesting how I have different bloodlines through the Arrows.
> On my mother's side was Baldwin Twins, and then on my
> grandma's side was all the way back to Stone Forehead.

William Red Hat Jr. had served in the U.S. Marines in the Vietnam War, and there had been terrible times in that conflict when
he called on the power of the Sacred Arrows to pull him through.
Having survived that war, and having seen the changes that had
come to the Cheyenne—northern and southern alike—William
Red Hat was able to comment on the difference between the ways
of the white majority and the Cheyenne minority:

> The People's way is a lot better than any governmental structure
> or any capitalist structure, because in the long run you benefit
> more from it. You don't get rich from it, but you have all the
> knowledge, all of what makes you who you are. . . . The govern-
> ment wants us to be capitalists. Okay, they make money, thieves,
> they steal money, so on and so forth. I mean, you can go on

down the line. So our Cheyenne people are just what the government wanted. They know how to steal money, they know how to use the loopholes, they know how to use the gray areas, so what are they talking about?

William Red Hat would agree that some Cheyenne had adjusted to the white person's way—sometimes with negative consequences—while others adhered to the old way, the one shown by Sweet Medicine. His own life reflected the tensions between Cheyenne and white society, but a photograph taken by his sister depicts him as a peaceful, contented man. Just as this book began with a visual image—the paintings by George Catlin of High-Backed Wolf and She-Who-Bathes-Her-Knees, it concludes with a visual.

In keeping with Cheyenne tradition, older members of the tribe pass Cheyenne culture and customs to the next generation. As the Cheyenne struggle to maintain their language, identity, and existence, many young members of the nation carry on the pride of their people.

William Red Hat and his wife stand with their faces to the camera. In the background is the summit of Noahvose, the Holy Mountain.

William Red Hat stands on the viewer's left. The hair on his forehead is still dark, but there is some white in his beard. He wears clothing that might be worn by any white American, but the position of the photograph, with the Holy Mountain in back, indicates his Native identity.

Nellie Red Hat is on the right. She wears glasses, and, like her husband, she is dressed in clothing, including a windbreaker, that almost any American—black, white, Hispanic, or other—might use today. She leans in toward her husband, who has his left arm around her.

William and Nellie Red Hat have made some compromises over the years. They have had to. The power of the Anglo-American majority, including its economic leverage, makes it nearly impossible for a Native person to live just as his or her ancestors did. The Red Hats have held onto their Cheyenne heritage. He is the Keeper of the Sacred Arrows, the bundle that ties The People to their earliest leader. They are a happy couple, blessed with children and a large extended family. Like The People of the nineteenth century—the ones whom George Catlin met in the summer of 1832—The People of today have made the adjustments necessary to live in the world created by the majority, all the while maintaining their traditional beliefs.

Chronology

YYYYYYYYYYYYY

pre-date   Sweet Medicine brings the Sacred Arrows to The People.

1650–1750   The Cheyenne move from the western Great Lakes area to the Great Plains.

1680   First meeting between the Cheyenne and white people (French-Canadian) occurs.

circa 1750   The Cheyenne obtain their first horses.

1804–1805   Explorers Meriwether Lewis and William Clark meet the Cheyenne.

Timeline

1650–1750
The Cheyenne move from the western Great Lakes area to the Great Plains

1820s
The Cheyenne divide into northern and southern sections

1851
The Fort Laramie Treaty (also known as Horse Creek) is signed

1700 1800

1680
First meeting between the Cheyenne and white people (French-Canadian) occurs

1825
First treaty between the Cheyenne and the United States is enacted

1854
The Plains Indian Wars begin

1820s	The Cheyenne divide into northern and southern sections.
1825	First treaty between the Cheyenne and the United States is enacted.
Circa 1830	The Cherokee lose the Sacred Arrows to the Pawnee.
1832	George Catlin paints High-Backed Wolf and She-Who-Bathes-Her-Knees.
1832	Bent's Fort is built in southern Colorado.
1833	Night the Stars Fell
1848	California Gold Rush spurs migration west.
1851	The Fort Laramie Treaty (also known as Horse Creek) is signed.
1854	The Plains Indian Wars begin.

1864
Sand Creek Massacre, in which a Colorado militia kills as many as 150 Cheyenne

1887
Indian General Allotment Act passes Congress

1924
All Native Americans become citizens, by act of Congress

1900   2000

1868
Battle of the Washita (also known as Massacre)—George Custer attacks a Cheyenne village, killing more than 100

1876
Custer's Last Stand at Little Bighorn

1934
The Indian Reorganization Act passes Congress

1970s
Northern Cheyenne resist Big Coal leases

1859	Silver is discovered in Colorado.
1861	The American Civil War begins.
1863	Cheyenne chiefs visit President Lincoln.
1864	Sand Creek Massacre, in which a Colorado militia kills as many as 150 Cheyenne.
1868	Battle of the Washita (also known as Massacre)—George Custer attacks a Cheyenne village, killing more than 100.
1874	Gold is discovered in the Black Hills.
1874	Violation of the Sacred Buffalo Hat
1876	Crook's Fight on the Rosebud; Custer's Last Stand at Little Bighorn.
1877	Cheyenne and Sioux surrender to U.S. Cavalry in large numbers.
1878	Northern Cheyenne exodus from Fort Reno.
1884	The Tongue River reservation is established by presidential order.
1887	Indian General Allotment Act passes Congress.
1894	The Sun Dance is prohibited.
1900	The Tongue River reservation is reconfirmed by presidential order.
1917	United States enters World War I; many Cheyenne enlist.
1924	All Native Americans become citizens, by act of Congress.
1925	Thomas B. Marquis arrives in Montana and begins to photograph Cheyenne.
1925	By this year, alcoholism becomes a significant problem among the Northern Cheyenne.
1934	The Indian Reorganization Act passes Congress.
1941	United States enters World War II; many Cheyenne serve overseas.
1945	Group of Cheyenne pray for peace on Bear Butte.

1959	The Sacred Buffalo Cap is opened in the presence of several white people.
1961	Bear Butte becomes a South Dakota state park.
1967	John Stands in Timber and Margot Liberty have their work published as *Cheyenne Memories*.
1969	Father Peter J. Powell's *Sweet Medicine* is published.
1970s	Northern Cheyenne resist Big Coal leases.
1978	Court rules in favor of Northern Cheyenne; coal leases are terminated.
1990s	Controversy begins over the Sturgis Motorcycle Rally.
2001	Dull Knife Memorial College is renamed Chief Dull Knife College.
2002	Jerry Mader's *The Road to Lame Deer* is published.
2006	Margot Liberty's *Northern Cheyenne Album* is published.

Glossary

Bear Butte   The Anglo-American name for the butte that the Cheyenne call *Noahvose* (the Holy Mountain where The People are taught).

Bent's Fort   The first Anglo-American fort, also trading post, in Cheyenne country. It was built in 1832.

Big Coal   A term used to describe the major U.S. coal companies.

Counting coup   Touching an enemy with a lance or a stick.

Erect Horns   The cultural hero of the Suhtai who brought the Sacred Buffalo Hat.

Exodus   A general term, referring to the escape, or movement of a people. In the case of the Cheyenne, it applies to the escape from Indian Territory in the autumn of 1878.

Great White Father   Indian name for the president of the United States.

Keeper   One of the most important and honored positions among The People, who kept the Sacred Arrows or the Sacred Buffalo Hat.

Lame Deer   Cheyenne town in southeastern Montana.

Night the Stars Fell   November 12–13, 1833. The Leonid meteor shower.

Pawnee   The most ancient foes of the Cheyenne.

(Four) Sacred Arrows   A gift from the gods, brought to the Cheyenne by Sweet Medicine sometime long in the past.

Sacred Buffalo Hat   A collection of materials that are kept in a bundle and only rarely opened for viewing.

Skidi   The Pawnee band that captured the Sacred Arrows in 1830.

Sturgis, South Dakota   The closest town to Bear Butte, Sturgis is best known for its popular motorcycle rally, the largest in North America.

Suhtai   A subgroup of the Cheyenne, they were once a separate people.

Sun Dance   A ceremony enacted by many Plains peoples. The Cheyenne form was banned by the U.S. government in 1894 but was later revived.

Sweet Medicine   The culture hero of the Cheyenne, who brought the Four Sacred Arrows from the Holy Mountain.

Bibliography

Alderson, Nannie T., and Helena Huntington Smith. *A Bride Goes West.* New York: Farrar & Rinehart, 1942.

Berthrong, Donald J. *The Cheyenne and Arapaho Ordeal: Reservation and Agency Life in the Indian Territory, 1875–1907.* Norman: University of Oklahoma Press, 1976.

Boye, Alan. *Holding Stone Hands: On the Trail of the Cheyenne Exodus.* Lincoln: University of Nebraska Press, 1999.

Fay, George E. *Treaties between the Tribes of the Great Plains and the United States of America: Cheyenne and Arapaho, 1825–1900.* Greeley: University of Northern Colorado, 1977.

Fowler, Loretta. *Tribal Sovereignty and the Historical Imagination.* Lincoln: University of Nebraska Press, 2002.

"A Great Indian Outbreak; Rapine and Murder in Kansas." *New York Times,* September 20, 1878.

Hatch, Thom. *Black Kettle: The Cheyenne Chief Who Sought Peace but Found War.* Hoboken, N.J.: John Wiley & Sons, 2004.

Hendricks, Stephen. "Small Wonder: A Northern Cheyenne Lawyer Defends Her Nation." *Sierra* 89 (2004): 18–22.

Hinz-Penner, Raylene. *Searching for Sacred Ground: The Journey of Chief Lawrence Hart, Mennonite.* Telford, Penn.: Cascadia Publishing House, 2007.

Hoig, Stan. *The Battle of the Washita: The Sheridan-Custer Indian Campaign of 1867–1869.* Lincoln: University of Nebraska Press, 1976.

Hutton, Paul Andrew, ed. *The Custer Reader.* Lincoln: University of Nebraska Press, 1992.

Hyde, George E. *A Life of George Bent: Written from His Letters.* Norman: University of Oklahoma Press, 1968.

Keizer, Garret. *The Unwanted Sound of Everything We Want: A Book About Noise.* New York: Public Affairs, 2010.

Matthiessen, Peter, editor. *George Catlin: North American Indians.* New York: Penguin Books, 1989.

Moore, John H. *The Cheyenne.* Malden, Mass.: Blackwell Publishers, 1996.

Nadeau, Remi. *Fort Laramie and the Sioux Indians.* Englewood Cliffs, N.J.: Prentice Hall, 1967.

Penoi, Charles. *No More Buffaloes.* Yukon, Okla.: Pueblo Press, 1981.

Philbrick, Nathaniel. *The Last Stand: Custer, Sitting Bull, and the Battle of the Little Bighorn.* New York: Viking, 2010.

Powell, Father Peter J. *The Cheyennes, Maheo's People: A Critical Bibliography.* Bloomington: Indiana University Press, 1980.

———. *Sweet Medicine: The Continuing Role of the Sacred Arrows, the Sun Dance, and the Sacred Buffalo Hat in Northern Cheyenne History.* Norman: University of Oklahoma Press, 1969.

Sandoz, Mari. *Cheyenne Autumn.* New York: McGraw-Hill, 1953.

Schlesier, Sibylle M., editor. *William Wayne Red Hat Jr: Cheyenne Keeper of the Arrows.* Norman: University of Oklahoma Press, 2008.

Stands in Timber, John, and Margot Liberty. *Cheyenne Memories.* New Haven, Conn.: Yale University Press, 1967.

Further Resources

YYYYYYYYYYYYYYYYYYYYYYYYYYY

Aadland, Dan. *Women and Warriors of the Plains: The Pioneer Photography of Julia E. Tuell.* Missoula, Mont.: Mountain Press Publishing Company, 2000.

Grinnell, George Bird. *The Cheyenne Indians: Their History and Lifeways, Illustrated.* Bloomington, Ind.: World Wisdom, 2008.

Liberty, Margot, editor. *A Northern Cheyenne Album,* with commentary by John Woodenlegs. Norman: University of Oklahoma Press, 2006.

Mader, Jerry. *The Road to Lame Deer.* Lincoln: University of Nebraska Press, 2002.

Nabokov, Peter. *Where the Lightning Strikes: The Lives of American Indian Sacred Places.* New York: Penguin Books, 2006.

Web Sites

Cheyenne and Arapaho Tribes
http://www.c-a-tribes.org

Homeland: Four Portraits of Native Resistance,
Katahdin Productions
http://katahdin.org/films/indian/intro.html

Interview with Dr. Margot Liberty, Friends of the
Little Bighorn Battlefield
http://www.Friendslittlebighorn.com/interviewmliberty.htm

Northern Cheyenne Tribe
http://www.cheyennenation.com

Protect Bear Butte: "Our Sacred Ground Is Not Your Playground"
http://protectbearbutte.com

The Sand Creek Massacre: The Making of a Documentary Film
http://www.manataka.org/page633.html

Smoke Signals: BLM Report on Northern Cheyenne
http://smokesignals2006blogspot.com/2006/11/blm-report-on-northern-cheyenne-by-joe.html

Picture Credits

Index

A

Adams, John Quincy, 34
alcoholism, 99, 102, 103
Alderson, Nannie T., 90–91
Alderson family, 87–88
Algonquin family, 30
Allen, Jay, 114–115
allotment, 89–90, 103
American Regular Army, 34
American-Cheyenne conflict, renewal of, 59
ancestral heritage, 105
ancestral homeland, 81
Anglo-American settlers, 54, 74, 87
Arapaho, 31, 35, 44, 45, 50, 103, 104
    first meeting with, 32
    Fort Lyon and, 56
Arizona, 46
Arkansas River, 45, 53
Arthur, Chester A., 87
Atkinson, Henry, 33, 34, 35, 48
attire, tribal, 118
automobiles, 97–98, 99

B

Baldwin Twins, 117
Balenti, Richard, 105
Battle of Ash Hollow, 49
Battle of Little Bighorn, 65, 68–72
Battle of the Washita, 61–62, 70, 71
Battle of the Washita, The (Hoig), 61, 62
Bear Butte, 24–26, 83. *See also* sacred mountain
belief system, 26, 32, 49
Bent, Charles, 38
Bent, George, 35, 36–37, 39, 52–53
Bent, William, 38, 39, 54
Bent family, 38–39, 52–53
Berthrong, Donald J., 91–92
Bighead, Kate, 70–71
Billings, Montana, 101
Black Hawk tribe, 48
Black Hills, 64, 66, 74, 80
Black Kettle (chief), 39, 50, 51, 53, 82
    Denver militia and, 56–57
    at Fort Lyon, 58
    hoisting American flag, 57, 58
    as peace chief, 53, 54
    scalping of, 60, 62
    village/band of, 61
Black Kettle (Hatch), 56, 57
Black Wolf, 88
Blackfeet, 14, 35, 46
bluecoats (U.S. soldiers), 43, 49
Bonnin, L.S., 104
Bougainville, 106
Boye, Alan, 82–83
Brewster, George, 87
Bride Goes West, A (Alderson), 87, 90–91
Bridge (medicine healer), 78
buffalo, 15, 23, 28, 54, 86–87, 109
Bull, 35, 36–37, 38
Bull Coming, Roy, 105
Bureau of Indian Affairs, 77, 81, 94
Bureau of Land Management, 111

C

Caddo, 50
Campbell, Joseph, 20
Canadian County, Oklahoma, 76
Carter, Jimmy, 116
Catlin, George, 14–15, 16, 17, 19, 118, 119
cattle, 87–89, 93, 96–97, 98, 100
census, 77
centennial year, 66
chastity, 33
Cheyenne, The (Moore), 105
Cheyenne and Arapaho Ordeal, The (Berthrong), 91–92
Cheyenne Autumn (Sandoz), 76, 78, 81
Cheyenne Indian War of 1864, 56
Cheyenne Memories (Liberty and Stands in Timber), 21, 22, 23, 26, 68
Cheyenne Social Club, The (film), 14
Cheyenne War of 1864, 54
Cheyennes, Maheo's People, The (Powell), 37
child rearing, 91
Chivington, John, 56, 57–58
citizenship, 96
Clark, William, 33
coal, discovery of, 110–113
Collier, John, 103

Colorado, 39, 46, 53–54, 56
Comanche, 50
Comes in Sight (chief), 68
Confederate States of America (CSA), 53
Council of 44, 27
counting coup, 17, 36, 49, 67, 69, 105
County Line, The, 115
courtship, 33
Crazy Horse (chief), 66, 74, 80
Cree, 14
Crook, George, 66
Crook's Fight, 67–68
Crow, 35, 44, 54, 69
Crow Indian Reservation, 87, 116
cultural force, 85, 110
Custer, George Armstrong
  as American war hero, 62, 66
  arrival in Great Plains, 59
  in the Black Hills, 64–66
  death of, 72, 74
  as foe of The People, 66
  Indian women and, 70–71
  Little Bighorn, 68–72
  massacre on the Washita, 61–62, 65
  winter campaign of, 59–61
Custer Reader, The, 70
Custer's Last Stand, 68, 69, 72, 98. *See
  also* Little Bighorn

D

Dakota Territory, 64
Dances with Wolves (film), 83
Dawes Act, 89
Declaration of Independence, 66
Denver, Colorado, 54, 55, 57
diabetes, 102
diet, 100–102, 103
Dives Backwards, Sam, 105
Dodge City, Kansas, 80
Dog Soldier Society, 27, 49, 54, 59, 96
drought, 102
Dull Knife (chief), 74, 82–83, 84
  exodus from Fort Reno, 78–81
  U.S. troops after, 81, 85
Dull Knife Memorial College, 101
Dust Bowl, 102–103

E

Earth Men (white peoples), 28
Eisenhower, Dwight D., 108
El Reno, Oklahoma, 105
elderly, hospitality to, 23
Elk Society, 27, 49
Erect Horns, 64
Evans, John, 54–56
Evanston, Illinois, 55
exile, return from, 26–27
exodus from Oklahoma, 76–85
  Dull Knife/Little Wolf, 78–81, 84

retracing trail, 82–83
split into two groups, 81
trip to Fort Reno, 76–77
U.S. troops after, 81, 84–85

F

face painting, 17, 18
"Fight Where We Lost the Black Hills," 74
Fighting Sixth, 56
Fillmore, Millard, 43
Fitzpatrick, Thomas, 43
Flowers, Betty Sue, 98
Fort Bent, 38–39, 56
Fort Keogh, 74
Fort Laramie, 40–51
  Horse Creek, 43–45
  Manifest Destiny (term), 41–43
  Northern/Southern Cheyenne, 46
  presents, wagonloads of, 44, 45
  shot heard over the Plains, 47–48
  treaty of, 44–45, 47
  violent attack near, 47–48
  warrior societies and, 49–51
Fort Lyon, 56, 58
Fort Reno, 76, 77, 78, 82
Fort Robinson, 83
Four Sacred Arrows. *See* Sacred Arrows
Fowler, Loretta, 104
Fox Society, 27, 49
French-Canadians, 38

G

George Catlin: North American Indians,
  15
Going Rogue (Palin), 101
gold, discovery of, 64, 66
Grant, Ulysses S., 63–64, 66, 85
Grattan, John L., 47–48
gray coats (U.S. negotiators), 43
Greaney, John, Jr., 105–106
Greasy Grass, the, 72
Great Depression, 99–102, 103
Great Lakes area, 28
Great Plains/Great Plains Indians, 36,
  59, 85
  diplomacy/warfare, 43
  grand council of tribes of, 44
  move to Great Plains, 28–29
Great Spirit, 51
Great War, 94, 95–97. *See also* World
  War I
"Great White Father," 34, 49, 50, 51, 81, 85

H

Harney, William S., 48–49
Hatch, Thom, 50, 53, 56, 57
Hayes, Rutherford B., 85
Hero with a Thousand Faces, The (Camp-
  bell), 20

High-Backed Wolf, 15–17, 16, 40, 46, 118
    scalp locks and, 16–17
    treaty signing by, 33–34, 35
history, early Cheyenne, 20–29
    exile, return from, 26–27
    move to Great Plains, 28–29
    sacred mountain, 24–26
    Sweet Medicine, 21–24
    tribal organization, 27–28
    water world, 20–21
Hoig, Stan, 61
*Holding Stone Hands: On the Trail of the
    Cheyenne Exodus* (Boye), 82
holy mountain. *See* sacred mountain
"honor" system, in war, 49
Horse Creek. *See* Fort Laramie
"horse people," 35
horses, 23, 28–29, 97–98

I

Indian agency, 78
Indian commissioners, 63
Indian General Allotment Act, 89
Indian Reorganization Act (IRA),
    103–104
Indian Territory, 53, 74, 81, 84, 88
Indian wars, 80
influenza epidemic, 96
Is'siwun, 66, 109. *See also* Sacred Buffalo
    Hat

J

Joseph (chief), 80

K

Kansas, 46
Keeper of the Sacred Arrows, 38, 40, 117,
    119
Keeper of the Sacred Hat, 32, 64–66
Keizer, Garret, 25, 114
Kiowa, 50

L

La Junta, Colorado, 38, 54
La Salle, Robert de, 30
Lame Deer (chief), 86
Lame Deer reservation, 82, 90
Lame Deer, village of, 86–87
Land Run of 1892, 92–93
language, loss of, 115
Last Bull, 109
Last Stand, The (Philbrick), 68
Leonid meteor shower, 18–19, 40
Lewis, Meriwether, 33
Liberty, Margot, 20
Life of George Bent, A, 35, 36–37, 40
Lincoln, Abraham, 50–51, 53, 55
Lincoln, Mary Todd, 50
Little Bighorn, 68–72

Custer, Indian women and, 70–71
    reaction to battle, 72, 74
    suicide boys/suicide dance, 68–69, 72
    troops/Indians, movements of, 73
Little Bighorn River, 73
Little Coyote, 109
Little Raven, Jr., 104
Little Wolf, 84–85
    Cheyenne groups divided, 81
    exodus from Fort Reno, 78–81
    retracing trail of, 82–83
    U.S. troops after, 81, 84
"Long Hair," 70

M

Maahotse, 37
Magpie, 39
Maheo (master of life), 26, 27, 117
Mandan, 14
Manifest Destiny (term), 41–43
Marquis, Thomas B., 70, 98–99
massacres, 57–58, 61–62, 65, 70, 84
McKinley, William, 89
medicine bundle, 109
Medicine Lodge, 58, 62
Me-o-tzi, 71
Mexico, 43
Miles, John D., 77
Miles, Nelson A., 74–75
military service, 95–96, 105–107
militiamen, 58
Minnesota, 21, 55
Missouri River, 66
Mitchell, David, 43
Montana, 32, 77, 82, 86, 87, 89, 112
    ranching experiment in, 93
    Sacred Buffalo Hat in, 46
Moore, John, 105
Morning Star Institute, 116
Mother Earth, 109
motorcycle rally, 25, 113–115
Moving Behind (Cheyenne woman), 62

N

Nadeau, Remi, 47–48
names for the Cheyenne, 19, 21
Native Action (film), 111
Native Action (non-profit), 113
Native American Church, 100
Navajo Code Talkers, 106
Nebraska, 44
New Mexico, 46, 53
New York Times, 80
Night the Stars Fell, the, 18–19, 40
Nighthorse Campbell, Ben, 116
Nightwalker, Roy, 105
Ni-oh-ma-até-a-nin-ya, 21
No More Buffaloes (Penoi), 97
Noahvose. See sacred mountain

Northern Cheyenne, 54, 86, 103
  cattle/land rights and, 94
  exodus from Fort Reno, 78–81
  flight of the, 31
  at Little Bighorn, 69, 72
  to Oklahoma reservation, 76–78, 79
  separation from Southern, 46, 47
  Sioux and, 64, 66, 68
  total defeat of, 74–75
  U.S. Cavalrymen and, 67
  war attitude of, 67
Northern Cheyenne Album, A, 99
Northern Cheyenne Reservation, 109,
  110–113
Northern Plains, 35, 78
Northern Plains Indians, 64
number four, as sacred, 24, 27

O

Oglala Sioux, 74
Oklahoma, 46, 53, 61, 74, 86, 93. *See also*
  Exodus from Oklahoma
oral tradition, 20
orphans, 44
Osage, Wesley, 105
Owl Woman, 39

P

Palin, Sara, 101
Panic of 1873, 64
Pawnee, 44, 46
  Sacred Arrows and, 37, 38, 39, 64, 117
  war with the, 35–37, 40
peace chiefs, 27, 41, 53, 54
peace pipe, 15, 16
Penoi, Charles, 97, 100–101
People, The, 19, 23, 26, 62
  in 1914, 93–94
  beliefs within, 49
  governing of, 27
  Maheo and, 117
  separation of, 46
People of the Great Plains, The, 19
Peoria, Illinois, 30
Philadelphia, Pennsylvania, 66
Philbrick, Nathaniel, 68
physical characteristics, 15
Pierce, Franklin, 48
Pike, Albert, 53
Plains Indian Wars, 57, 63
Plains Indians, 49, 60–61, 67
Platte River, 45
Polk, James K., 42, 43
Powell, Peter J., 37, 108–109, 110
Prohibition, 99

R

railroad, 59
Rankin, Jeanette, 95

Red Bute, 45
Red Hat, Nellie, 119
Red Hat, William Wayne, Jr., 117–119
Red Power, 110, 116
Red Shield Society, 27
Regular Army, 49
religion. *See* belief system
Rendlebrock, Joseph, 77, 79–80
Reno, Marcus, 72
Republic of Mexico, 43
Republican River, 49, 49–51
reservations. *See also* specific reservation
  allotment, 89–90
  Black Hills and, 64
  land runs and, 92–93
  the north, 86–89
  The People in 1914, 93–94
  the south, 90–93
  sovereignty and, 108
Road to Lame Deer, The (Flowers), 98
Rocky Mountains, 45
Roosevelt, Franklin D., 103
Rosebud River, 67–68

S

Sacred Arrows, 27, 32, 35, 115–116,
  117–119
  captured by Pawnee, 37, 64
  location of, 46, 91, 93
  in Oklahoma, 46
  "replacement" arrows, 40
Sacred Buffalo Hat, 32, 91
  damage to, 64–66
  safekeeping of, 46, 93
  symbolism/ritual, 109–110, 115–116
sacred mountain, 24–26, 64, 83, 107, 119.
  See also Bear Butte
  motorcycle rally and, 25, 113–115
Sand Creek, 56
Sand Creek massacre, 57–58
  Black Kettle and, 57, 58, 60, 61
  Dog Soldiers and, 59
Sandoz, Mari, 76, 78, 81
Santa Fe, New Mexico, 38
Santee Sioux, 54, 55
scalps/scalping, 16–17, 44, 60, 67, 109
Schlesier, Sibylle M., 117
scouts, 69, 78, 96
Selective Service, 96
Seminole, 48
separation, northern/southern sections,
  46
Sheridan, Philip, 59, 61
Sherman, William T., 60, 61
She-Who-Bathes-Her-Knees, 17–18, 71,
  118
Shoshone, 44
shot heard over the Plains, 47–48
Shown Harjo, Susan, 116

Sioux, 14, 44, 64
   cow capture/bloodbath, 47–48
   at Little Bighorn, 69, 72
   Northern Cheyenne and, 66, 68
   Santee Sioux, 54, 55
   total defeat of, 74–75
Sitting Bull (chief), 66, 74
Slim Buttes, 74
Small, Gail, 111, 112–113
Snake, 44
Society of Friends (Quakers), 63
Sootkis, Andrew, 82–83
South Dakota, 24–25, 46, 77, 113–115
Southern Cheyenne, 54, 86
   land situation of, 92–93, 103
   separation from Northern, 46, 47
Southern Plains, 79
sovereignty, 108
"Spanish Flu," 96
spiritual power. *See* Sacred Arrows
Spotted Blackbird, 72
Spotted Elk, Sam, 83
Standing Elk (chief), 75
Stands in Timber, John, 115
   book excerpts, 20–21, 28–29, 32, 67,
      68–69, 72, 87
   father of, 89
Stone Forehead, 117
Sturgis, South Dakota, 25, 113–115
Suhtai, the, 32–33
Suhtaio, the, 109
suicide dance/oaths, 67, 68–69, 72
Sumner, E.V., 49
Sun Dance, Cheyenne, 21
Sweet Medicine, 21–24, 41, 112, 118
   exile and, 23, 26–27
   miracles performed by, 22
   predictions of, 27–28, 29
   roles/vanishing of, 23–24
   Sacred Arrows and, 27, 37, 40
   sacred mountain and, 24–26, 117
   teachings of, 26–27, 89
   unforgiveable act of, 23
   war and, 38
Sweet Medicine (Powell), 109

T

Teaching Place, 83
telegraph, advent of, 48
Termination Era, 108–109
Terry, Alfred, 66
Tongue River, 87
Tongue River reservation, 89, 93, 99
tradition, continuation of, 115–116
Transcontinental Railroad, 59
Treaty of Fort Laramie, 44–45, 47
treaty of July 6, 1825, 33–34

tribal lands, shrinking of, 53
tribal organization, 27–28
*Tribal Sovereignty and the Historical
   Imagination* (Fowler), 104
"Twenties, Roaring," 98–99

U

United States
   increase in size of, 43
   right to establish posts, 45
*Unwanted Sound of Everything We Want,
   The* (Keizer), 25, 114–115
U.S. Army, 49, 96
U.S. Cavalrymen, 14, 15, 59
   7th Cavalry, 60, 65, 74
   in centennial ceremonies, 66
   kill-or-be-killed attitude of, 67
U.S. Civil War, 39, 53, 58–59
   massacre by militiamen, 57, 58
   Union/Confederacy, 51, 52, 55
U.S. troops, numerical superiority of, 49

V

virtues, key, 23
vision, dragonflies and, 83
voyageurs, 38

W

War Between the States, 52
warbonnets, 67
warrior society, 15, 27, 49–51, 95, 105
Washington, D.C., 50–51, 56, 63, 77, 89,
   94, 103
Washita River, 60, 61–62, 65
Wayne, John, 14
Wessels, Henry, 85
"Where the Girl Saved Her Brother,"
   67–68
White House, 50, 63
white peoples, 28, 47, 54, 74, 87. *See also*
   "Great White Father"
White River, 74
White Thunder, 40
Wilson, Woodrow, 94, 96
Wolf on the Hill. *See* High-Backed Wolf
women/*female* power, 32, 109
Women's Army Corps, 106
Wooden Leg, 100
Woodenlegs, John, 100–101, 109, 112,
   115
World War I, 95–97
World War II, 104–105, 108
Wyoming, 29, 30, 44, 46

Y

Yellowstone River, 66

About the Contributors

Ť Ť Ť Ť Ť Ť Ť Ť Ť Ť Ť Ť Ť Ť

SAMUEL WILLARD CROMPTON has been interested in Native Americans ever since he visited Old Deerfield and the reconstructions of a Mohawk encampment at Lake George, New York, as a teenager. Today he teaches history at Holyoke Community College in western Massachusetts and writes for the teenage audience, with a special focus on cultural topics. He wrote *The Mohawk* for Chelsea House and is the editor of *Illustrated Atlas of Native American History*.

Series editor **PAUL C. ROSIER** received his Ph.D. in American History from the University of Rochester in 1998. Dr. Rosier currently serves as Associate Professor of History at Villanova University (Villanova, Pennsylvania), where he teaches Native American History, American Environmental History, Global Environmental Justice Movements, History of American Capitalism, and World History.

In 2001, the University of Nebraska Press published his first book, *Rebirth of the Blackfeet Nation, 1912–1954*; in 2003, Greenwood Press published *Native American Issues* as part of its Contemporary Ethnic American Issues series. In 2006, he coedited an international volume called *Echoes from the Poisoned Well: Global Memories of Environmental Injustice*. Dr. Rosier has also published articles in the *American Indian Culture and Research Journal*, the *Journal of American Ethnic History*, and *The Journal of American History*. His *Journal of American History* article, entitled "They Are Ancestral Homelands: Race, Place, and Politics in Cold War Native America, 1945–1961," was selected for inclusion in *The Ten Best History Essays of 2006–2007*, published by Palgrave MacMillan in 2008; and it won the Western History Association's 2007 Arrell Gibson Award for Best Essay on the history of Native Americans. His latest book, *Serving Their Country: American Indian Politics and Patriotism in the Twentieth Century* (Harvard University Press), is winner of the 2010 Labriola Center American Indian National Book Award.